Comparative Reading

Recent Titles in
Bibliographies and Indexes in Education

Integrating Women's Studies into the Curriculum: An Annotated Bibliography
Susan Douglas Franzosa and Karen A. Mazza, compilers

Teacher Evaluation and Merit Pay: An Annotated Bibliography
Elizabeth Lueder Karnes and Donald D. Black, compilers

The Education of Poor and Minority Children: A World Bibliography,
Supplement, 1979-1985
Meyer Weinberg, compiler

Comparative Reading

An International Bibliography

Compiled by
John Hladczuk
and
William Eller

Bibliographies and Indexes in Education, Number 4

Greenwood Press
New York • Westport, Connecticut • London

Library of Congress Cataloging-in-Publication Data

Hladczuk, John.
  Comparative reading.

  (Bibliographies and indexes in education,
ISSN 0742-6917 ; no. 4)
  Bibliography: p.
  Includes index.
  1. Reading—Bibliography. I. Eller, William.
II. Title. III. Series.
Z5818.L3E4 1987   [LB1050]   016.4284   87-25407
ISBN 0-313-26004-4 (lib. bdg. : alk. paper)

British Library Cataloguing in Publication Data is available.

Library of Congress Catalog Card Number: 87-25407
ISBN: 0-313-26004-4
ISSN: 0742-6917

First published in 1987

Greenwood Press, Inc.
88 Post Road West, Westport, Connecticut 06881

Printed in the United States of America

The paper used in this book complies with the
Permanent Paper Standard issued by the National
Information Standards Organization (Z39.48-1984).

10 9 8 7 6 5 4 3 2 1

For

Mom and Dad,
Sharon
and
Adam, Jason and A.J.

Contents

Acknowledgments

We would like to thank Mary Sive, Loomis Mayer, Carol and Richard Norris, and Sharon Hladczuk in helping us bring the bibliography to its final form.

Comparative Reading

1

Comparative Reading:
An Introduction

Every bibliography is, to some extent, self-explanatory. The germ
of the concept is often captured with the most cursory of examinations.
Then, all that is left to do is to ascertain the "voice" of that
particular bibliography.

The "voice" of this bibliography is the voice of expansion,
flexibility, latitude- of change. Change in the sense of moving away
from a rigid definition of what comparative reading is or ought to be.

Among the entries that follow there is to be found research that
fulfills the most strict of "comparative reading" definitions. On the
other hand, there are entries that obviously do not. What we have
attempted to achieve is a cross-section of entries of an inter-
disciplinary nature.

Thus, one will find entries relating to the social, historical,
philosophical, economic, psychological, political, anthropological and
theoretical aspects of reading.

This is done for two major reasons. The first is to encourage and
stimulate a wide range of divergent research and analysis in reading.
The second reason is to provide a basis for the possible applicability--
in whole, part or adaptation--of some of the findings herein.

This bibliography is not exhaustive. For some topics it may not
even be representative. We have not, to any great extent, for example,
despite the fact that they are closely related to reading, dealt with
the topics of literacy and illiteracy. We believe that their essences
are distinct enough so as to remain conceptually discrete.

We also assume that anyone led to this bibliography is already
familiar with the summaries of investigations relating to reading (1925
to present), over time, from the pens of William S. Gray, Helen Robinson
and Sam Weintraub, et al. Thus, they will not be found as entries.

Further, as a qualifying note, section 2.C. 'National Research,' should not be understood in a strict geopolitical/diplomatic/U.N. represented way. Rather, it is more a classifying scheme for reading research.

Organization of the Book

The organization of the book is oriented around two primary areas. The first area is International Research. This is further divided into three divisions, entitled, (1) Cross-Cultural Research; (2) World Regional Research; and (3) National Research.

The second area is what we describe as involving the correlates of reading. The act of reading is co-related with certain other significant and logical phenomena. These co-related phenomena are: (1) Comparison (Chapter III); (2) Learning to Read (Chapter IV); (3) Basic Skills (Chapter V); (4) Language (Chapter VI); (5) Culture (Chapter VII); (6) The Organization of Reading (Chapter VIII); (7) The Improvement of Reading (Chapter IX); (8) Evaluation and Research in Reading (Chapter X); (9) The Psychology of Comparative Reading (Chapter XI); and (10) General Reading (Chapter XII).

In summary, our goal has been to expose and thus stimulate any user of this book to a myriad of ways of conceptualizing, analyzing and researching the phenomenon known as reading.

2

International Research

A. CROSS-CULTURAL RESEARCH

2.A.1. Boucherant, Elisabeth. "International Cooperation and The Improvement of Reading." In Reading: What of the Future? pp. 286-292. Edited by Donald Moyle. London: United Kingdom Reading Association, 1975.

2.A.2. Bulcock, Jeffrey W., et al. Reading Competency as a Predictor of Scholastic Performance: Comparisons Between Industrialized and Third-World Nations. Paper presented at the Annual Meeting of the International Reading Association World Congress on Reading. Singapore: n.p., 1976. ED 136 221.

2.A.3. Carneal, Ann S. An International View of Primary Reading Practices. N.P.: n.p., 1977. ED 162 282.

2.A.4. Carver, Ronald P. "How Good Are Some of the World's Best Readers?" Reading Research Quarterly 20, 4 (Summer 1985): 389-419.

2.A.5. Coleman, James S. "Methods and Results in the IEA Studies of Effects of School on Learning." Review of Educational Research 45, 3(Summer 1975): 355-386.

2.A.6. Collins, Cathy. "When Reading Instruction Begins and Is Tested in 25 Countries that use an Alphabetic Language System." Reading Horizons 22, (Fall 1981): 7-15.

2.A.7. Collins, Cathy, and Demos, Elene S. "An International Study of the Elements of Beginning Reading Instruction." The Reading Teacher 36, 8(April 1983): 814-818.

2.A.8.   Collins, Cathy, and Demos, Elene S.   "Trends and Needs in
            Beginning Reading Instruction 14 Countries."   The
            Reading Teacher 36, (May 1983):   900-904.

2.A.9.   Committee on the Professional School and World Affairs.
            The Professional School and World Affairs.
            Albuquerque, New Mexico: The University of New Mexico
            Press, 1968.

2.A.10.   Cummings, James.   "A Comparison of Reading Achievement in
            Irish and English Medium Schools."   In Studies in
            Reading, pp. 128-133.   Edited by Vincent Greaney.
            Dublin: The Educational Company, 1977.

2.A.11.   DeLandsheere, Aletta Grisay, and Georges, Henry.   "High
            Achievers in Belgium: A Partial Analysis of I.E.A.
            Science Literature and Reading Comprehension Data."
            Comparative Education Review 18, 2(June 1974):
            188-195.

2.A.12.   Douglass, Malcolm P.   "Research Around the World."   In
            The 44th Yearbook of the Claremont Reading Conference.
            Edited by Malcolm P. Douglass.   Claremont, California:
            Claremont Reading Conference, 1980.

2.A.13.   Downing, John.   A Cross-National Investigation of Cultural
            and Linguistic Mismatch in Fourteen Countries.   Paper
            presented at the World Federation for Mental Health,
            Anniversary World Mental Health Congress.   Sydney:
            n.p., 1973.   ED 095 493.

2.A.14.   Downing, John.   "Cross-National Comparisons of Reading
            Achievement."   In Comparative Reading, pp. 32-64.
            Edited by John Downing.   New York: Macmillan, 1973.

2.A.15.   Downing, John.   "Cultural Expectations."   In Comparative
            Reading, pp. 105-127.   Edited by John Downing.   New
            York: Macmillan, 1973.

2.A.16.   Downing, John, ed.   The First International Reading
            Symposium.   London: Cassell.   New York: Day, 1966.

2.A.17.   Downing, John, and Brown, Amy L., eds.   The Second
            International Reading Symposium.   London: Cassell,
            1967.

2.A.18.   Downing, John, and Brown, Amy L., eds.   The Third
            International Reading Symposium.   London: Cassell,
            1968.

2.A.19.   Elder, Richard D.   "Oral Reading Achievement of Scottish
            and American Children."   Elementary School Journal 71,
            4(January 1971):   216-320.

2.A.20.   Faunce, Wilhelmina.   "Reading Around the World."   Reading
            Horizons 9, 1(1968-1969):   29.

2.A.21.   Feitelson, Dina, ed. **Cross-Cultural Perspectives on
           Reading and Reading Research.** Newark, Delaware:
           International Reading Association, 1978.

2.A.22.   Fitzgerald, Thomas P., and Fitzgerald, Ellen F. "A Cross
           Cultural Study of Three Measures of Comprehension at
           the Primary and Intermediate Levels." **Educational
           Research Quarterly** 3, 2(Summer 1978):   84-92.

2.A.23.   Flanagan, John C. "Changes in School Levels of
           Achievements: Project TALENT Ten and Fifteen Year
           Retests." **Educational Research** 5(September 1976):
           9-12.

2.A.24.   Fleming, James T. **On the International Need for the
           Advanced Study of Reading.** Paper presented at the
           Annual Meeting of the Reading Association of Ireland.
           Dublin: n.p., 1976. ED 137 743.

2.A.25.   Foshay, Arthur W.; Thorndike, Robert L.; Hotyat, Fernand:
           Pidgeon, Douglas A.; and Walker, David A. **Educational
           Achievements of Thirteen-Year-Olds in Twelve
           Countries.** Hamburg: UNESCO Institute for Education,
           1962.

2.A.26.   Fry, Edward. "Reading Improvement Courses in the United
           States and Africa." **Teacher Education** 5(February
           1965):   204-208.

2.A.27.   Gloger, M. Ted. **An Observation of Reading Programs Within
           Selected Countries Around the World.** Paper presented
           at the Annual Convention of the International Reading
           Association. New Orleans: n.p., 1974.

2.A.28.   Grant, Barbara M. **Literacy Through Literature: A Cross-
           Cultural and Broad-Spectrum Approach to Reading and
           Writing Facility Through Literature.** Paper presented
           at the New Jersey Reading Teachers Association
           Conference. McAfee, New Jersey: n.p., 1978. Ed 163
           467.

2.A.29.   Gray, William S. "Current Reading Problems: A World
           View." **Education Digest** 21(1955):   28-31.

2.A.30.   Greaney, Vincent, and Neuman, Susan B. "Young People's
           Views of the Functions of Reading: A Cross-Cultural
           Perspective." **The Reading Teacher** 37, 2(November
           1983):   158-163.

2.A.31.   Greenberg, Nancy M., ed. **Other Lands, Other Peoples: A
           Country by Country Fact Book.** Washington, D.C.:
           National Education Association, Committee on
           International Relations, 1969. ED 040 115.

2.A.32.   Grundin, Hans U., et al. "Cloze Procedure and
           Comprehension: An Exploratory Study Across Three

Languages." Journal of Research in Reading 4, 2(September 1981): 104-122.

2.A.33.   Hansen, Philip A., and Hansen, Shirley B. Mainstreaming Across Nations. Paper presented at the Annual Meeting of the Claremont Reading Conference. Claremont, California: n.p., 1979. Ed 167 985.

2.A.34.   Henry, J. A. "A Cross-national Outline of Education." Current Anthropology 1(1960): 267-305.

2.A.35.   Hochberg, Julian, and Brocks, Virginia. "Reading as an International Behavior." In Theoretical Models and Processes of Reading. Second Edition. Edited by H.S. Singer and R. B. Ruddell. Newark, Delaware: International Reading Association, 1976.

2.A.36.   Hood, Joyce, and Gonzales, Clara R. The Oral Reading of Colombia Second-and Fourth-Graders: An Illustration of Issues in Cross-Cultural Oral Reading Research. N.P.: n.p., 1976. ED 130 226.

2.A.37.   Husen, Torsten. "Introduction to the Reviews of Three Studies of the International Association for the Evaluation of Educational Achievement (IEA)." American Educational Research Journal 11, 4(Fall 1974): 407-408.

2.A.38.   Husen, Torsten. Multi-national Evaluation of School Systems. Paris: UNESCO International Institute for Educational Planning, 1975.

2.A.39.   Husen, Torsten. "Evaluation Reflections: Policy Implications of the IEA Findings and Some of Their Repercussions on National Debates on Educational Policy." Studies in Educational Evaluation 3(Summer 1977): 129-141.

2.A.40.   Husen, Torsten. "Are Standards in U.S. Schools Really Lagging Behind Those in Other Countries?" Phi Delta Kappan, 7(March 1983): 455-461.

2.A.41.   International Association for the Evaluation of Educational Achievement. IEA Six-Subject Survey Instruments: English as a Foreign Language Tests. Stockholm: n.p., 1975. ED 102 181.

2.A.42.   International Association for the Evaluation of Educational Achievement. IEA Six-Subject Survey Instruments: French as a Foreign Language Tests. Stockholm: n.p., 1975. ED 102 184.

2.A.43.   International Association for the Evaluation of Educational Achievement. IEA Six-Subject Survey Instruments: Stage 2 Manuals. (Science, Reading Comprehension, and Literature). Stockholm: n.p.,

1975. Ed 102 193.

2.A.44.   International Association for the Evaluation of
            Educational Achievement. IEA Six-Subject Survey
            Instruments: Teacher Questionnaire: Mother Tongue
            (Reading Comprehension and Literature). Stockholm:
            n.p., 1975. ED 102 174.

2.A.45.   International Association for the Evaluation of
            Educational Achievement. IEA Six-Subject Survey
            Instruments: Student Reading Comprehension
            Questionnaire. Stockholm: n.p., 1975. Ed 102 173.

2.A.46.   International Association for the Evaluation of
            Educational Achievement. IEA Six-Subject Survey
            Instruments: Reading Comprehension Tests. Stockholm:
            n.p., 1975. Ed 102 172.

2.A.47.   Jenkinson, Marion D. Reading Instruction, An
            International Forum: Proceedings. Newark, Delaware:
            International Reading Association, 1967.

2.A.48.   Johnson, Dale D. "Sex Differences in Reading Across
            Cultures." Reading Research Quarterly 9, 1(1973-74):
            67-86.

2.A.49.   Johnson, Dale D. An Investigation of Sex Differences in
            Reading in Four English Speaking Nations. Madison,
            Wisconsin: Research and Development Center for
            Cognitive Learning, 1972.

2.A.50.   Johnson, Dale D. "Cross Cultural Perspectives on Sex
            Differences in Reading." The Reading Teacher 29,
            8(May 1976): 747-752.

2.A.51.   Johnson, J. David, and Tims, Albert R. Magazine
            Evaluations and Levels of Readership: A Cross-
            Cultural Analysis. Paper presented at the Annual
            Meeting of the Association for Education in
            Journalism. Seattle, Washington: n.p., 1978. Ed 168
            050.

2.A.52.   Jones, Earl, ed. Intercultural Education Series.
            Selected Latin American Literature for Youth. College
            Station, Texas: Bryan Independent School District,
            Texas A&M University, 1968. Ed 052 098.

2.A.53.   Karlsen, Bjorn. "Reading Difficulties Throughout the
            World." The Reading Teacher 9 2(December 1955):
            99-101.

2.A.54.   Kenworthy, Leonard S. The International Dimension of
            Education. Washington, D.C.: National Education
            Association, Association for Supervision and
            Curriculum Development, 1970.

2.A.55.   Kimura, Yuko, and Bryant, Peter. "Reading and Writing in
            English and Japanese: A Cross-Cultural Study of Young
            Children." British Journal of Educational Psychology
            1, 2(June 1983): 143-153.

2.A.56.   King, Kenneth, ed. Literacy Research in Developing
            Countries. Final Report. Bonn: German Foundation
            for International Development; Ottawa: Education,
            Science and Documentation Division, International
            Development Research Center, 1978. Ed 178 896.

2.A.57.   Kline, Carl L., and Lee, Norma. "A Transcultural Study of
            Dyslexia: Analysis of Reading Disabilities in 425
            Chinese Children Simultaneously Learning to Read and
            Write in English and in Chinese." Bulletin of the
            Orton Society 19(1969): 67-81.

2.A.58.   Kline, Carl L., and Lee, Norma. "A Transcultural Study of
            Dyslexia: Analysis of Language Disabilities in 277
            Chinese Children Simultaneously Learning to Read and
            Write in English and in Chinese." Journal of Special
            Education 6(1972): 9-26.

2.A.59.   Kritzer, Richard. The Application of Videotape to the
            Teaching of Reading: Implications for Global
            Education. Hicksville, New York: Exposition Press,
            1976.

2.A.60.   Kugelmass, S., and Lieblich, A. "Impact of Learning to
            Read on Directionality in Perception: A Further Cross
            Cultural Analysis." Human Development 22, 6(1979):
            406-415.

2.A.61.   Laubach, Frank C. Teaching the World to Read. London:
            United Society for Christian Literature, 1948.

2.A.62.   Legrand, Louis. "European Research Policies: Analysis of
            Sixteen Country Reports." Western European Education
            6, 3(Fall 1974): 63-90.

2.A.63.   Lindgren, Scott D., et al. "Cross-National Comparisons of
            Developmental Dyslexia in Italy and the United
            States." Child Development 56, 6(December 1985):
            1404-1417.

2.A.64.   Lloyd, B.A., and Lloyd, Rosalie. "A Comparison of the
            Reading Readiness and Mental Maturity Scores of
            Selected First Grade Pupils in an American School and
            in a Belgian School: A Pilot Study." Journal of the
            Reading Specialist 7(1967): 14-17, 25.

2.A.65.   Malmquist, Eve. "Teaching of Reading: A Worldwide
            Concern." In Reading and Inquiry. Edited by J.
            Allen Figurel. Newark, Delaware: International
            Reading Association, 1965.

2.A.66.   Malmquist, Eve. "Some Studies on Reading Disabilities in
            Various Countries. From Psychological and
            Physiological Aspects of Reading. A Report of the
            Twenty-Fourth Annual Conference and Course on Reading.
            July 8-19, 1968. School of Education, University of
            Pittsburgh.

2.A.67.   Malmquist, Eve. "Reading: A Human Right and a Human
            Problem." In Reading: A Human Right and a Human
            Problem, pp. 1-8. Edited by Ralph C. Staiger and
            Oliver Andresen. Newark, Delaware: International
            Reading Association, 1969.

2.A.68.   Malmquist, E. "Role of IRA in Raising Reading Standards
            Around the World." International Reading Association
            Conference Proceedings 13, Part 1. 1969, 832-840.

2.A.69.   Malmquist, Eve. Developing Reading Ability - A Worldwide
            Challenge: The Present Situation and an Outlook for
            the Future. Linkoping, Sweden: Linkoping University,
            Department of Education, Report No. ISBN-91-7372-456-
            4; LIU-PEK-R-68. 1981. ED 208 341.

2.A.70.   Matejcek, Z. "Dyslexia: An International Problem." The
            Bulletin of the Orton Society 18(1968): 13.

2.A.71.   McCullough, Constance M., et al. "Discussion Review of
            Reading Comprehension Education in Fifteen Countries."
            American Educational Research Journal 11, 4(Fall
            1974): 409-414.

2.A.72.   Mialaret, Gaston. World Survey of Pre-School Education.
            Paris: UNESCO; New York: Distributed by Unipub,
            1976.

2.A.73.   National Society for the Study of Education. The United
            States and International Education. Edited by Harold
            G. Shane. Chicago: The University of Chicago Press,
            1969.

2.A.74.   Noonan, Richard D. School Resources, Social Class, and
            Student Achievement: A Comparative Study of School
            Resource Allocation and the Social Distribution of
            Mathematics Achievement in Ten Countries. Stockholm:
            Almqvist & Wiksell International; New York: J. Wiley,
            1976.

2.A.75.   Ollila, Lloyd O., ed. Beginning Reading Instruction in
            Different Countries. (World Congress on Reading, 7th,
            Mamburg, 1978). Newark, Delaware: International
            Reading Association, 1981.

2.A.76.   Peaker, Gilbert F. An Empirical Study of Education in
            Twenty-One Countries: A Technical Report.
            International Studies in Evaluation VIII. Stockholm:
            International Association for the Evaluation of

Educational Achievement, 1975. Ed 117 125.

2.A.77.   Porter, D. "Six Area Studies." Comparative Education
           7, 1(August 1971): 15-20.

2.A.78.   Postlethwaite, T. Neville. Some General Findings from the
           IEA Surveys in Science, Reading Comprehension, and
           Literature. Paper presented at the American
           Educational Research Association Meeting. New
           Orleans: n.p., 1973. Ed 079 191.

2.A.79.   Postlethwaite, T. Neville. A selection from the Overall
           Findings of the I.E.A. Study in Science, Reading
           Comprehension, Literature, French as a Foreign
           Language, English as a Foreign Language and Civic
           Education. IIEP Occasional Papers No. 30. Paris:
           United Nations Educational, Scientific and Cultural
           Organization, International Institute for Educational
           Planning, 1976. ED 133 107.

2.A.80.   Postlethwaite, T. N., ed. "International Project for the
           Evaluation of Educational Achievement (IEA)."
           International Review of Education 15 2(1969):
           131-204.

2.A.81.   Postlethwaite, T. Neville, ed. "What Do Children Know?
           Comparative Education Review. International Studies
           on Educational Achievement." Comparative Education
           Review 18, 2(June 1974).

2.A.82.   Purves, Alan C., et al. Reading and Literature: American
           Achievement in International Perspective. Urbana,
           Illinois: National Council of Teachers of English,
           1981. ED 199 741.

2.A.83.   Robinson, Gail L. Language and Multicultural Education:
           An Australian Perspective. Sydney: Australia and
           New Zealand Book Co., 1978.

2.A.84.   Robinson, H. Alan, et al. "Beginning Readers' Concept of
           Reading: An International Survey." Reading—Canada—
           Lecture 2, 1(January 1983): 12-17.

2.A.85.   Robinson, H. Alan, et al. Expressed Reading Interests of
           Young Children: An International Study. Paper
           presented at the International Reading Association
           World Congress on Reading. Vienna: n.p., 1974.
           ED 096 614.

2.A.86.   Robinson, Richard D.; Goodacre, Elizabeth J.; and McKenna,
           Michael C. "Psycholinguistic Beliefs: A Cross-
           Cultural Study of Teacher Practice." Reading
           Improvement 15, 2(Summer 1978): 134-157.

2.A.87.   Sartain, Harry W. Mobilizing Family Forces for World-
           wide Reading Success. Newark, Delaware:

International Reading Association, 1981.

2.A.88.   Sheridan, E. Marcia. Ideographs, Syllabaries, and
           Alphabets: Reading as Information Processing in
           Different Writing Systems. 1979. ED 192 263.

2.A.89.   Shuy, R. W. "Some Language and Cultural Differences in
           a Theory of Reading." In Psycholinguistics and the
           Teaching of Reading. Edited by K. S. Goodman and
           J. T. Fleming. Newark, Delaware: International
           Reading Association, 1969.

2.A.90.   Staiger, Ralph C., and Andresen, Oliver. Reading: A
           Human Right and A Human Problem. Newark, Delaware:
           International Reading Association, 1969.

2.A.91.   Steffensen, Margaret S. Register, Cohesion, and Cross-
           Cultural Reading Comprehension. Technical Report
           No. 220. Cambridge, Massachusetts and Urbana,
           Illinois: Bolt, Beranek and Newman, Inc. and Illinois
           University, Center for the Study of Reading, 1981.
           ED 253 697.

2.A.92.   Stevenson, Harold W., et al. "Reading Disabilities: The
           Case of Chinese, Japanese, and English." Child
           Development 53, 5(October 1982): 1164-1181.

2.A.93.   Stevenson, Robert L. "Cross-Cultural Validation of
           Readership Prediction Technique." Journalism
           Quarterly 50(Winter 1973): 690-696.

2.A.94.   Strickland, Dorothy S., ed. The Role of Literature in
           Reading Instruction: Cross-Cultural Views. Newark,
           Delaware: International Reading Association, 1981.
           ED 199 692.

2.A.95.   Taiwo, Oladele. "Cultural Relevance of Reading
           Materials." In Reading: What of the Future? pp. 261-
           266. Edited by Donald Moyle. London: United Kingdom
           Reading Association, 1975.

2.A.96.   Tarnopol, Lester, and Tarnopol, Muriel. "Reading and
           Learning Problems Worldwide." In Reading
           Disabilities: An International Perspective, pp. 1-
           26. Edited by Lester Tarnopol and Muriel Tarnopol.
           Baltimore, Maryland: University Park Press, 1976.

2.A.97.   Tarnopol, Lester, and Tarnopol, Muriel. Reading
           Disabilities: An International Perspective.
           Baltimore, Maryland: University Park Press, 1976.

2.A.98.   Tarnopol, Muriel. "Reading Problems Worldwide." Bulletin
           of the Orton Society 27(1977): 102-111.

2.A.99.   Thorndike, Robert L. Reading Comprehension Across
           National Boundaries. N.P.: n.p., 1972. ED 064 351.

2.A.100.   Thorndike, Robert L. **Reading Comprehension Education in
            Fifteen Countries: An Empirical Study.** New York:
            Wiley, 1973.

2.A.101.   Tordrup, S.A. "Laeseudviklingen Hos Elever Med Store Lae
            Sevansk Eligheder (An Investigation of Reading
            Progress Among Pupils with Major Reading
            Difficulties)." **Skolepsykologi** 4(1967): 3.

2.A.102.   Tyler, Ralph W. "The U.S. vs. the World: A Comparison of
            Educational Performance." **Phi Delta Kappan** 62,
            5(January 1981): 307-310.

2.A.103.   UNESCO. **Literacy and Education for Adults.** Paris:
            UNESCO, 1964.

2.A.104.   Walker, D. A. **The IEA Six-Subject Survey: An Empirical
            Study of Education in Twenty-one Countries.** N.P.:
            Almqvist and Wiksell, 1976.

2.A.105.   White, W. "Dyslexia--Across Three Continents."
            Austrialian Journal of Remedial Education 7, 3(1975):
            13-18.

2.A.106.   Wilberg, J. Lawrence, and Blom, Gaston E. "A Cross-
            National Study of Attitude Content in Reading
            Primers." **International Journal of Psychology**
            5(1970): 109-122.

2.A.107.   World Congress on Reading, 3d, Sydney, 1970. **Improving
            Reading Ability Around the World.** Edited by Dorothy
            Kendall Bracken and Eve Malmquist. Newark, Delaware:
            International Reading Association, 1971.

2.A.108.   **World Survey of Education II.** Paris: UNESCO, 1958.

2.A.109.   **World Survey of Education III.** New York: Columbia
            University Press, 1961.

B. WORLD REGIONAL RESEARCH

1. Africa

2.B.110.   Fry, Edward. See entry 2.A.26.

2.B.111.   Jordan, R. R. "Reading Interests of Lower Secondary-
            School Children in Africa and Asia." **English Language
            Teaching Journal** 32, (January 1978): 143-151.

2.B.112.   McSwain, Martha I. B. "Opportunities to Use Family
            Resources for Reading in the Developing Countries of
            Africa." In **Mobilizing Family Forces for Worldwide
            Reading Success,** pp. 19-34. Edited by Harry W.
            Sartain.

2.B.113.   O'Halloran, George. "Indigenous Literacy Among the
            Mandinko of West Africa." **Journal of Reading** 22,
            6(March 1979):   492-497.

2.B.114.   Osa, O. "The Socio-Cultural Context of African Children's
            Reading Today." **Reading Improvement** 23 (Fall 1986):
            194-196.

2.B.115.   Yoloye, E. Ayotunde. "Readability Indices in the
            Evaluation of Curriculum Materials." **Journal of
            Curriculum Studies** 7, 1(May 1975):   78-84.

        2. Arab States

2.B.116.   McCrummen, Norman Henry III. "A Review of the Arab
            States' Training Centre's Programs of Fundamental
            Education, Community Development, and Functional
            Literacy." **Dissertation Abstract** V37(12), Sec. A.,
            P7490, 1976.

        3. Asia

2.B.117.   Jordan, R. R. See Section 2.B.1. entry no. 111.

2.B.118.   Kim, Byong Won, ed. **Reading English in Asia.** The First
            Yearbook of Literacy and Languages in Asia. Seoul,
            Korea: Literacy and Languages in Asia, 1984.

2.B.119.   Lee, Grace E. **Reading for Asian Students.** Northridge,
            California: California State University, 1976.
            ED 159 585.

2.B.120.   Lee, Grace E. "The Asian Connection." In **The 40th
            Yearbook of the Claremont College Reading Conference.**
            Edited by Malcolm P. Douglass. Claremont, California:
            Claremont Reading Conference, 1976.

2.B.121.   Valdenhuesa, Manuel E. "Publishing for New Literates in
            Asia." **Journal of Reading** 28, 7(April 1985):   632-
            634.

        4. Europe

2.B.122.   Malmquist, Eve. "A Decade of Reading Research in Europe,
            1959-1969: A Review." **Journal of Educational
            Research** 63, 7(1970):   309-329.

2.B.123.   Newcombe, Norman. **Europe at School.** London: Methuen,
            1977.

2.B.124.   Tuunainen, Karl, and Chiaroni, Alain, eds. Full
            Participation. Proceedings of the Second European
            Conference on Reading, Joensuu, 2-5 August 1981,

Finland. Joensuu, Finland: University of Joensuu, 1982.

2.B.125.   Wollner, M. H. B. "Reading for Meaning in European Schools." **Education** 76, (May 1956): 530-535.

5. Latin America

2.B.126.   Spaulding, Seth Joseph. "An Investigation of Factors Which Influence the Effectiveness of Fundamental-Education Reading Materials for Latin-American Adults. (Volumes I and II)." Dissertation Abstracts, V20(06), P2106, 1953.

6. Scandinavia

2.B.127.   Copp, Barrie R. "Reading as Viewed by Our Eastern European Colleagues." **Journal of Reading** 13, 6(March 1970): 441-446.

2.B.128.   Malmquist, E. "Reading Research in Scandanavia." In **Reading and Inquiry, Proceedings of the International Reading Association,** pp. 399-404. Edited by J. A. Figurel. 1965.

7. Socialist Countries

2.B.129.   Anweiler, Oskar. "Toward a Comparative Study of the Education Systems in Socialist Countries of Europe." **Comparative Education** 11(March 1975): 3-11.

8. Southeast Asia

2.B.130.   Karim, Yaakub Bin. "Opportunities to use Family Resources for Reading in Developing Countries of Southeast Asia." In **Mobilizing Family Forces for Worldwide Reading Success,** pp. 35-43. Edited by Harry W. Sartain. Newark, Delaware: International Reading Association, 1981.

9. Western Europe

2.B.131.   Bamberger, Richard. "Developing Lifelong Reading Interests and Reading Habits." **Bookbird** 10, 2(1972): 28-31.

C. NATIONAL RESEARCH

1. Argentina

2.C.132.   Boland S. "The Place of Teaching Reading in the Buenos
             Aires Curriculum." Australian Journal of Reading 2
             (June 1983):   79-81.

2.C.133.   Cossettini, Olga. El Lenguaje U La Escritura En Primer
             Grado (Language and Writing in the First Grade)."
             Buenos Aires: Editorial Universitaria De Buenos
             Aires, 1961.

2.C.134.   Dezeo, Emilia C., and Muniz, Juan M. La Ensenanza Del
             Lenguaje Grafico (The Teaching of the Written
             Language). Buenos Aires: Edit. Ferrari Hermanos,
             1936, p. 279.

2.C.135.   Filho, Lourenco. ABC Tests, 6th Edition. Buenos Aires,
             Argentina: Editorial Kapelusz, 1962, p. 30.

2.C.136.   Gorriti, Carlos J. Robles, and Muniz, Ana M. Rodriquez.
             "Learning Problems in Argentina." In Reading
             Disabilities: An International Perspectives, pp. 27-
             37. Edited by Lester Tarnopol and Muriel Tarnopol.
             Baltimore, Maryland: University Park Press, 1976.

2.C.137.   Lopez de Nelson, Ernestina. Veo Y Leo. Buenos Aires:
             Coni Hermanos, undated.

2.C.138.   Mercante, Victor. "Como Seaprende A Leer." ("How One
             Learns to Read."). Achrivas De Ciencias De La
             Educacion (La Plata, 6) (1919):   328.

2.C.139.   Onativia, Oscar V. Metodo Integral Para La Ensenanza De
             La Lectoescritura Inicial (Integrated Method for the
             Teaching of Reading and Writing to Beginners). Buenos
             Aires: Editorial Humanitas, 1967.

2.C.140.   Perelstein de Braslavsky, Berta. "Metodos De Ensenanza De
             Lectura Y Dislexias" ("Methods in the Teaching of
             Reading and Dyslexias"). Fenoaudiolofica 3(1961),
             publication of the ASALFA.

2.C.141.   Perelstein de Braslavsky, Berta. La Querella De Los
             Metodos En La Ensenanza De La Lectura (The Dispute
             Over Methods in the Teaching of Reading). Buenos
             Aires: Editorial Kapelusz, 1962.

2.C.142.   Perelstein de Braslavsky, Berta. "Argentina." In
             Comparative Reading, pp. 259-284. Edited by John
             Downing. New York: Macmillan, 1973.

2.C.143.   Sastre, Marcos. Anagnosia, 3rd Edition. Buenos Aires:
             Gobierno De La Provincia De Buenos Aires, 1852;
             Ferreyra Andres, El Nene, Buenos Aires: A. Estrada

Y Cia. Undated.

2. Armenia

2.C.144.   Hildreth, Gertrude. "Armenian Children Enjoy Reading."
            The Reading Teacher 19(March 1966): 433-445.

3. Australia

2.C.145.   Andrews, Robert John. The Reading Attainments of Primary
            School Children in Three Queensland Schools. St.
            Lucia, Queensland, Australia: University of
            Queensland Press, 1964.

2.C.146.   "Around Australia: Involving Parents in the Reading
            Program." Australian Journal of Reading 4, 4(November
            1981): 206-210.

2.C.147.   Bourke, Sid, et al. "Australian Studies in Student
            Performance--1980." Australian Journal of Reading 5,
            1(March 1982): 37-41.

2.C.148.   Boyd, R. M. "The Aboriginal Child and Literacy."
            Aboriginal Child at School 6, 5(October/November
            1978): 3-9.

2.C.149.   Broadby, F. M. 1979 Survey of Basic Reading Skills of 14
            Year Old Tasmanian Students. Hobart, Tasmania:
            Education Department. Research Branch, 1980.

2.C.150.   Broadby, F. M. 1981 Survey of Basic Rading Skills of 10
            Year Old Tasmanian Students. Hobart, Tasmania:
            Education Department. Research Branch, 1982.

2.C.151.   Broadby, F. 1984 Survey of Basic Reading Skills of 10
            Year Old Tasmanian Students. Hobart, Tasmania:
            Education Department. Executive Support Services,
            1985.

2.C.152.   Buschenhofen, D. "Adapting Reading Methodology to
            Aboriginal Children." Aboriginal Child at School 10,
            5(October/November 1982): 3-11.

2.C.153.   Cambourne, B., and Rousch, P. "How do Australian Children
            Read? The Riverina Research Studies." Reading
            Education 5, 1(Autumn 1980): 5-17.

2.C.154.   Campbell, A., and Spearritt, D. Measuring Reading Compre-
            hension in the Upper Primary School. Canberra:
            Australian Government Publishing Service, 1977.

2.C.155.   Coppell, B. "The Murawian Readers--A First Report on the
            Development of Community Related Curriculum
            Materials." Reading Education 3, 2(Spring 1978):
            27-30.

2.C.156.   Coppell, W. G. "The Murawina Readers—A First Stage in
             the Development of Community Related Curriculum
             Materials in an Aboriginal Context." **Aboriginal Child
             at School** 7, 1(February 1979): 47–51.

2.C.157.   Corcoran, W. T. "Indoctrination in Literature: Some
             Australian Evidence." **English in Australia** 53
             (September 1980): 50–59.

2.C.158.   Davidson, G. "Learning to Read the Aboriginal Way."
             Reading Education 8, 1(Autumn 1983): 5–16.

2.C.159.   Downing, J., and Morris, B. "An Australian Program for
             Improving High School Reading in Content Areas."
             Journal of Reading 28, (December 1984): 237–243.

2.C.160.   Duck, G. **A Comparison of the Standards of Educational
             Achievement of Queensland Year 7 Pupils in 1972 and
             1977.** Brisbane: Queensland, Department of Education,
             Research Branch, 1978.

2.C.161.   Duck, Greg. **A Comparison of the Reading Achievement of
             Queensland Year 5 Pupils Between 1971 and 1977.**
             Brisbane: Research Branch, Department of Education,
             1979.

2.C.162.   Dwyer, B., and Dwyer, J. "Australian Reading: Are
             Standards Declining? No." **The Reading Teacher** 33,
             (November 1979): 152–154.

2.C.163.   Elkin, J. "Reading Disability Research in Australia."
             Slow Learning Child 22, 2(July 1975): 109–119.

2.C.164.   Freebody, Peter, and Rust, Patricia A. "Predicting Read-
             ing Achievement in the First Year of Schooling: A
             Comparison of Readiness Tests and Instructional
             Programs." **Journal of School Psychology** 23, 2(Summer
             1985): 144–155.

2.C.165.   Gale, M. A. "Phonics for the Aboriginal Classroom."
             Aboriginal Child at School 10, 5(October/November
             1982): 32–37.

2.C.166.   Hagger, T. Dudley. "Learning Disabilities in Australia."
             In **Reading Disabilities: An International
             Perspective,** pp. 39–66. Edited by Lester Tarnopol
             and Muriel Tarnopol. Baltimore, Maryland: University
             Park Press, 1976.

2.C.167.   Horner, Jim, and Moore, Frances. "Research into Reading:
             A Study of Reading in Transition Between Primary and
             Secondary Schools in Tasmania." **English in Australia**
             58(December 1981): 43–61.

2.C.168.   Jacobson, J., ed. **A Summary of the Research into Reading
             Standards of Queensland Grade Five Pupils 1933–1977.**

          Brisbane: Queensland Institute for Educational
          Research, 1978.

2.C.169. January, G. R. "Developing a Set of Readers for
          Aboriginal Children." **Aboriginal Child at School**
          6, 5(October/November 1978): 32-34.

2.C.170. Jones, D. "The Effects of Teacher Style on Year One Ab-
          original Children's Reading Achievement." **Aboriginal
          Child at School** 7, 3(June 1979): 48-58.

2.C.171. Kindt, I. **Reading in Queensland Primary Schools--Manage-
          ment and Methodology.** Brisbane, Queensland: Depart-
          ment of Education, Curriculum Branch, 1980.

2.C.172. Lipscombe, R., and Burnes, D., eds. **Aboriginal Literacy:
          Bridging the Gap.** Adelaide: Australian Reading
          Association, 1982.

2.C.173. Marshall, May F. "Countdown to Reading." In **Reading: A
          Human Right and a Human Problem**, pp. 29-33. Edited
          by Ralph C. Staiger and Oliver Andresen. Newark,
          Delaware: International Reading Association, 1969.

2.C.174. McBride, B.; Phillips, K.; and Byrne, M. **A Comparison of
          the Reading Achievement of Queensland Year 5 Pupils
          Between 1971, 1976 and 1981.** Brisbane: Department of
          Education, Research Branch, 1982.

2.C.175. McEvoy, Kathy. "Special Needs of Aboriginal in the Teach-
          ing of Reading." **Australian Journal of Reading** 8, 2
          (March 1985): 39-43.

2.C.176. Morris, A., and Cope, r. G. "Preparation of Australian
          Primary Teachers in the Teaching of Reading." **South
          Pacific Journal of Teacher Education** 6, 1(1978): 69-
          73.

2.C.177. Page, Glenda; Elkins, John; and O'Connor, Barrie, eds.
          **Communication Through Reading. Diverse Needs:
          Creative Approaches.** N.P.: Australian Reading
          Association, 1979.

2.C.178. Parke, M. B. "Invisible Reading Class in Australia's Out-
          back." **The Reading Teacher** 18, (November 1964): 124-
          127.

2.C.179. Pidgeon, Douglas A. "A Comparative Study of Basic Attain-
          ments." **Educational Research** 1(1958): 50-68.

2.C.180. Power, Colin. "Reaction to a Report on Reading
          Standards." **Australian Journal of Reading** 2(June
          1979): 92-95.

2.C.181. Rado, M. "The Language of Instruction of Immigrant
          Children: An Australian Solution." **International**

Review of Education 24, 3(1978):   415-418.

2.C.182.   Reeves, Noelene. "Teaching Convicts to Read in Colonial
            Australia." **Australian Journal of Reading** 6, (June
            1983): 65-72.

2.C.183.   Robinson, Gail L. See entry 2.A.83.

2.C.184.   Rothman, Sheldon L. "Reading Instruction in New South
            Wales Schools 1975-1900." **Reading Education** 7,
            1(Autumn 1982): 17-24.

2.C.185.   Salmond, J. "Aboriginals and Reading." **Aboriginal Child
            at School** 5, 5(October/November 1977): 57-63.

2.C.186.   South Australian Education Department. **Survey of Reading
            and Reading Procedures in Grade 3 Classes in Schools
            of the South Australian Education Department, 1972-
            1973.** Adelaide: n.p., 1973.

2.C.187.   Tobin, Barbara. "Leading Children to Pleasure Reading:
            the Role of the West Australian Young Readers' Book
            Award." **Australian Journal of Reading** 9, 2(June
            1986): 95-100.

2.C.188.   Watson, K. "The Reading Habits of Secondary School Pupils
            in New South Wales." **Orana** 15, 3(August 1979): 117-
            123.

2.C.189.   Watts, G. H., and McGaw, B. "Innovation and Research in
            Education." **Australian Journal of Education** 20,
            2(June 1976): 231-236.

2.C.190.   Western Australia Council for Special Education. **The
            Education of Children with Special Reading
            Disabilities in Western Australia: Report to the
            Minister of Education.** Perth: Western Australia
            Council for Special Education, 1984.

    4. Austria

2.C.191.   Bamberger, Richard, and Rabin, Annette T. "New Approaches
            to Readability: Austrian Research." **The Reading
            Teacher** 37, (February 1984): 512-519.

2.C.192.   Bamberger, Richard. "The Joy of Reading." In **Reading: A
            Human Right and a Human Problem**, pp. 125-129. Edited
            by Ralph C. Staiger and Oliver Andresen. Newark,
            Delaware: International Reading Association, 1969.

2.C.193.   Kowarik, Othmar. "Reading-Writing Problems in Austria."
            In **Reading Disabilities: An International
            Perspective**, pp. 67-83. Edited by Lester Tarnopol
            and Muriel Tarnopol. Baltimore, Maryland: University
            Park Press, 1976.

2.C.194.   Lanzelsdorfer, F., and Pacolt, E. **Wiener Kinder Lesen.**
            Vienna: Verlag Fur Jugend Und Volk, 1969.

5. Bahrain

2.C.195.   **Development of Education in Bahrain (1975-1976).** Bahrain:
            Ministry of Education, 1977. ED 144 896.

6. Bangladesh

2.C.196.   University of Dacca. Centre for Urban Studies. **Reading
            Habits in Dacca City, 1976: Preliminary Report.**
            Prepared by the Centre for Urban Studies, Department
            of Geography, University of Dacca. Sponsored by The
            National Book Centre, Bangladesh. Dacca: National
            Book Centre, Bangladesh, 1977.

7. Belgium

2.C.197.   De Landsheere, Aletta Grisay, et al. See entry 2.A.11.

2.C.198.   Klees, Marianne. "Learning Disabilities in Belgium." In
            Reading Disabilities: An International Perspective,
            pp. 85-96. Edited by Lester Tarnopol and Muriel
            Tarnopol. Baltimore, Maryland: University Park
            Press, 1976.

2.C.199.   Lloyd, B. A., et al. See entry 2.A.64.

8. Brazil

2.C.200.   Chesterfield, R. "Effects of Environmentally Specific
            Materials on Reading in Brazilian Rural Primary
            Schools." **The Reading Teacher** 32, (December 1978):
            312-315.

2.C.201.   Keithahn, L. "Teaching Reading in Brazil." **The Reading
            Teacher** 16, (September 1962): 2-6.

2.C.202.   Lopes-Correa, A. "MOBRAL: Participation-Reading in
            Brazil." **Journal of Reading** 19, (April 1976): 534-
            539.

9. Canada

2.C.203.   Barik, Henri C.; Swain, Merrill; and Gaudino, Vincent A.
            "A Canadian Experiment in Bilingual Schooling in the
            Senior Grades: The Peel Study Through Grade 10."
            Revue Internationale de Psychologie Appliquee 25
            (October 1976): 99-113.

2.C.204.   Barrieau, D. M. "Ivan Reads." Journal of the B.C.
            (British Columbia) English Teachers' Assocation 15,
            (June 1975): 61-63.

2.C.205.   Berger, A. "A Comparative Study of Reading Improvement
            Programs in Industry and Education in the United
            States and Canada." In Reading: Process and
            Pedagogy. Nineteenth Yearbook of the National Reading
            Conference. Edited by G. B. Schick and M. M. May.
            1970.

2.C.206.   Foster, Marion E., and Black, Donald B. "A Comparison of
            Reading Achievement of Christchurch, New Zealand and
            Edmonton, Alberta Public School Students of the Same
            Age and Number of Years of Schooling." Alberta
            Journal of Educational Research 11(March 1965): 21-
            31.

2.C.207.   Froese, Victor. "Trends in Canadian Provincial Reading
            Assessments." The English Quarterly 16, 4(Winter
            1984): 4-9.

2.C.208.   Gazean, Sonja, and MacIntyre, Robert. "Reading Help for
            New Canadians." Orbit 7, 5(December 1976): 9.

2.C.209.   Gunderson, Lee. "A Survey of L2 Reading Instruction in
            British Columbia." Canadian Modern Language
            Review 42, 1(October 1985): 44-55.

2.C.210.   Hayward F. M. "Reading and Study Instruction in Canadian
            Universities and Colleges." Journal of Reading 15,
            (October 1971): 27-29.

2.C.211.   Hummel, Jeffrey W. "Normative Data for Eight Dimensions of
            Reading Attitudes: Canadian Public School Students."
            Psychology in the Schools 21, 4(October 1984): 433-
            436.

2.C.212.   Hunter, William J.; Tan, Meng H.; and Wentzell, Sharon L.
            "The Effects of Fluctuations in Blood Glucose Levels
            on Reading Test Performance." School Psychology
            International 4, 3(July/September 1983): 153-157.

2.C.213.   Knights, Robert M; Kronick, Doreen; and Cunningham, June.
            "Learning Disabilities in Canada: A Survey of
            Educational and Research Programs." In Reading
            Disabilities: An International Perspective, pp. 97-
            114. Edited by Lester Tarnopol and Muriel Tarnopol.
            Baltimore, Maryland: University Park Press, 1976.

2.C.214.   Philion, William L. E., and Galloway, Charles, G. "Indian
            Children and the Reading Program." Journal of Reading
            12, 7(April 1969): 553-560.

2.C.215.   Stachelek, Deborah Ann. A Comparative Study of the
            Reading Interests of Grade 12 Students in Selected

Canadian and American Schools. New Britain,
Connecticut: Central Connecticut State College, 1976.
ED 141 793.

2.C.216.   Tashow, Horst G. "Inner City Canadian Native and Non-
Native Pupils' Achievement in Reading, Writing, and
Speaking." The Reading Teacher 34, 7(April 1981):
799–803.

2.C.217.   Thomas, R., et al. "Effective Early Reading Program."
Orbit 9, (June 1978): 14–15.

2.C.218.   Vancouver Remedial Reading Teachers' Association. Report
on the Survey of Remedial Reading Programs in British
Columbia Schools. Vancouver: British Columbia
Teachers' Federation, 1972.

2.C.219.   Walker, Laurence. "Newfoundland Dialect Interference in
Fourth Grade Spelling." CORE 3, 2(June 1979): On
No. 10 of 15 microfiches (26 frames).

2.C.220.   Yearwood, D. B., and Yearwood, E. I. Selectability of
Printed Materials in Support of the Grades 10 and 11
Social Studies Curriculum. Vancouver: Educational
Research Institute of British Columbia, 1979. ED 180
926.

10.   China

2.C.221.   Biyin, Zhang. "The Psychology of Reading in China."
School Psychology International 6, 1(January/March
1985): 30–33.

2.C.222.   Butler, Susan Ruth. "Reading Problems of Chinese
Children." In Reading Disabilities: An International
Perspectives, pp. 115–130. Edited by Lester Tarnopol
and Muriel Tarnopol. Baltimore, Maryland: University
Park Press, 1976.

2.C.223.   Ching, Ti. "Publish More and Better Self-Education
Readers for Young People." Chinese Education 9,
3(Fall 1976): 68–77.

2.C.224.   Dai, Bao-Yun and Lu, Ji-ping. "Reading Reform in Chinese
Primary Schools."   Prospects 15, 1(1985): 103–110.

2.C.225.   Dengler, Mary. What Children Read in China. Occasional
Paper No. 77-6. Stony Brook, New York: American
Historical Association, Faculty Development Program,
1977. ED 141 243.

2.C.226.   Erickson, D.; Mattingly, I. G.; and Turvey, M.T.
"Phonetic Activity in Reading: An Experiment with
Kanji." Haskins Laboratories Status Report on Speech
Research SR-33, 1972, 137–156.

2.C.227.   "Establish Theory Study Session for Cadres and Train
            Theory Tutors." Chinese Education 10, 1(Spring 1977):
            60-64.

2.C.228.   "Extracts from Post-Cultural Primers Reproduced by the
            Guomindang." Chinese Education 10, 2(Summer 1977):
            100-102.

2.C.229.   "Introduction: Primary-School Texts and Teaching Methods
            in the Wake of the Cultural Revolution." Chinese
            Education 10, 2(Summer 1977): 4-29.

2.C.230.   Jiang, Shanye, and Li, Bo. "A Glimpse at Reading
            Instruction in China." The Reading Teacher 38, 8
            (April 1985): 762-766.

2.C.231.   "Notes on the Use of Phonetics in Chinese Reading
            Primers." Chinese Education 10, 2(Summer 1977): 30-
            34.

2.C.232.   Pape, Lillie. "Reading Instruction in Modern China." The
            Reading Teacher 35, 6(March 1982): 688-694.

2.C.233.   Rosenbaum, L. "Chinese Education: Reading, Rote, and
            Regimentation." Yearbook (Claremont Reading
            Conference) 1983: 110-117.

2.C.234.   "Selections from the Grade-One Primary-School Primer of
            Guangdong Province, Used in the 1975-76 School Year."
            Chinese Education 10, 2(Summer 1977): 35-77.

2.C.235.   "Selections from the Elementary-School Readers Used in the
            Left-Wing Private Schools of Macau During 1975-1976."
            Chinese Education 10, 2(Summer 1977): 78-99.

2.C.236.   Sutton, Andrew. "Acupuncture and Deaf-Mutism- An Essay
            in Cross Cultural Defectology." Educational Studies
            2, 1(March 1977): 1-10.

2.C.237.   Swetz, Frank J., ed. "Popular Science Readers: an Aid
            for Achieving Scientific Literacy in the PRC."
            Chinese Education 11, 1(Spring 1978): 2-106.

    11. Colombia

2.C.238.   Hood, Joyce, et al. See entry 2.A.36.

    12. Cuba

2.C.239.   Bond, Burtis. "Some Aspects of Educating the Cuban
            Refugee Student." Clearing House 38(October 1963):
            77-79.

2.C.240.   Kozol, Jonathan. "How Cuba Fought Illiteracy." **Learning**
           5, (May–June 1977): 26–29.

2.C.241.   Lopez, J. "Preschool Reading Readiness Program." Journal
           of Reading 25, (December 1981): 234–240.

2.C.242.   Martuza, Victor R. "Evaluation of Reading Achievement in
           Cuban Schools: A Comparative Perspective." The
           Reading Teacher 40, 3(December 1986): 306–313.

2.C.243.   Pollack, Cecilia, and Martuza, Victor. "Teaching Reading
           in The Cuban Primary Schools." Journal of Reading 25,
           3(December 1981): 241–250.

    13. Czechoslovakia

2.C.244.   Kucera, O.; Matejcek, Z.; and Langmeier, J. "Dyslexia in
           Children in Czechoslovakia, 1963." American Journal
           of Orthopsychiatry 33: 448.

2.C.245.   Matejcek, Z. "The Care of Children with Reading
           Disability in Czechoslovakia." The Bulletin of the
           Orton Society 15(1965): 24.

2.C.246.   Matejcek, Zdenek. "Dyslexia in Czechoslovakian Children."
           In Reading Disabilities: an International
           Perspective, pp. 131–154. Edited by Lester Tarnopol
           and Muriel Tarnopol. Baltimore, Maryland: University
           Park Press, 1976.

2.C.247.   Zlab, Z. "Zkusenosti S Tridami Pro Dyslekticke Deti V
           Praze. (Experiences with Classes for Dyslexic
           Children in Prague.)." Otasky Defektol. 5(1969):
           169.

    14. Denmark

2.C.248.   Blake, M. E. "Reading in Denmark: A Relaxed Atmosphere
           Is the Key." The Reading Teacher 38, (October 1984):
           42–47.

2.C.249.   Ellehammer, M. "Reading Ability of Retarded Children."
           Educational Forum 19, (March 1955): 293–299.

2.C.250.   Engberg, Eva. "Mogens Jansen: An Interview with a Danish
           Reading Educator." The Reading Teacher 38, 4(January
           1985): 396–399.

2.C.251.   Florander, J. "Udbyttet Af Laesetraening." ("The Results
           of a Training Course in Reading.") Laesepoedagagen 18
           (1970): 55–83.

2.C.252.   Hermann, K. Reading Disability. Copenhagen: Munksgaard,
           1959.

2.C.253.   Jansen, M. "Two Essential Problems in Language Teaching."
            International Reading Association Conference Proceed-
            ings 13, Part 1, 1969, 856–863.

2.C.254.   Jansen, M. et al. "Reading Instruction in Danish
            Schools." The Reading Teacher 33, (October 1979):
            15–20.

2.C.255.   Jansen, M. "The Scope of Reading in Scandanavia." In
            Reading Instruction: An International Forum. Edited
            by M. D. Robinson. Newark, Delaware: International
            Reading Association, 1966.

2.C.256.   Jansen, M. "Hvor Laenge Vil Vi Blive Ved Med At Vente Pa
            Den Store Groeskarmand?" Skandinavisk Tidskrift For
            Laspedagoger 2(1968): 6–13. (Available in English
            under title, "How Long Will We Go on Waiting for the
            Great Pumpkin?").

2.C.257.   Jansen, M. "A Discourse on the Formulation of
            Registration Form–Danish." In Mirrors for Behavior,
            Vol. X. Edited by A. Simon and E. G. Boyer.
            Philadelphia, Pennsylvania: Research for Better
            Schools, Inc., 1970.

2.C.258.   Jansen, Mogens. "Denmark." In Comparative Reading, pp.
            285–307. Edited by John Downing. New York:
            Macmillan, 1973.

2.C.259.   Jansen, Mogens. The Teaching of Reading – Without Really
            Any Method: An Analysis of Reading Instruction in
            Denmark. Copenhagen: Munksgaard; Atlantic Highlands,
            New Jersey: Humanities Press, 1978.

2.C.260.   Jansen, Mogens. The Continued Need for Effective Remedial
            Reading Programs. Paper presented at the Annual
            Meeting of the International Reading Association. St.
            Louis: n.p., 1980. ED 189 545.

2.C.261.   Jansen, M., and Mylov, P. "Om Illustrationer I Danske
            Laeseboger, 1.–7. Skolear." ("An Illustration of
            Danish Readers for Grades 1–7."). Nordisk Tidskrift
            for Specialpedagogik 47(1969): 3–35.

2.C.262.   Jansen, Mogens; Soegard, Arne; Hansen, Mogens; and
            Glaesel, Bjorn. "Special Education in Denmark." In
            Reading Disabilities: An International Perspective,
            pp. 155–174. Edited by Lester Tarnopol and Muriel
            Tarnopol. Baltimore, Maryland: University Park
            Press, 1976.

2.C.263.   Jansen, M., et al. "New Cities, Educational Traditions
            and the Future." In Education in Cities. Edited by
            J. A. Lauwerys and D. Scanlon. London: The World
            Year Book of Education, 1970.

2.C.264.   Larsen, A. "Materiale Til Undervisning Af Ordblinde Og
            Laesesvage." ("Material for Instruction of the Word-
            Blind and Retarded Readers."). Laesepaedagogen
            1(1952): 13-15.

2.C.265.   Larsen, C. A. Om Undervisning Af Born Med Laese-og stave-
            Vanskeligheder I de Forste Skolear (On the
            Instruction of Children Encountering Difficulties in
            Reading and Spelling During the First Few Grades).
            Copenhagen: Danmarks Paedagogiske Institute (The
            Danish Institute for Educational Research), 1960.

2.C.266.   Low, A. "Soft Start of the Danish Schools: Learning to
            Read; Slowly." Claremont Reading Conference Yearbook
            43, 1979, 92-97.

2.C.267.   Lundahl, F. Laesepaedagogens Materiale- Og
            Frilaesningsliste (Laesepaedagogen's List of
            Educational Material and Free Reading). 7th Revised
            Edition. Dragor: Landsforeningen Af Laesepaedagoger,
            1969.

2.C.268.   Rasborg, F. "Om Muligheder For At Konstatere En Behandlings-
            effekt Hos Laeseretarderede" ("On the Possibilities
            of Ascertaining any Effect from the Remedial Teaching
            of Retarded Readers"). In Paedagogiskpsykologiske
            Tekster, Bind 2. Forskningsmetodologi (Texts on
            Educational Psychology, Vol. 2, Research Methodology).
            Copenhagen: Akademisk Forlag, 1966.

2.C.269.   Tordrup, S. A. "Stavefejl Og Fejltyper Hos Elever Fra 5.
            Normalklasse Og Fra 5. Og 6. Laeseklasse (Spelling
            Errors and Types of Errors Made by Pupils from the
            5th Normal Grade and the 5th and 6th Reading
            Classes)." Skolepsykologi 2(1965): 1-69, 75-91.

2.C.270.   Tordrup, S. A. "Laeseudviklingen Hos Elever Med Stove
            Laesevanskeligheder (The Development of Reading Among
            Pupils Experiencing Heavy Difficulties in Reading)."
            Skolepsykologi 4(1967): 1-154.

    15. Ecuador

2.C.271.   Maas-de Brouwer, T. A., and Samson-Sluiter, D. M. M.
            "Some Remarks About the Testing of Reading in a
            Foreign Language." Reading 12, 3(December 1978): 31-
            35.

    16. Egypt

2.C.272.   Al-Ahram Center for Scientific Translations. Selected
            Bibliography of Egyptian Educational Materials, Vol.
            6, No. 1, 1980. Cairo, Egypt: Al-Ahram Center for
            Scientific Translations, 1981. ED 210 227.

17. England/United Kingdom

2.C.273.   Anderson, Irving H., and Geraldine T. Scholl. "Comparison
            of the Reading and Spelling Achievement and Quality of
            Handwriting of Groups of English, Scottish and
            American Children: Summary of Research Completed
            Under Cooperative Research Project No. 1163." Ann
            Arbor, Michigan: n.p., 1962. ED 003 313.

2.C.274.   Baird, C. L. "The Role of the Teacher of Six-and Seven-
            Year-Old Children." British Journal of Educational
            Psychology 38(1968): 323-324.

2.C.275.   Bentley, Diana, and Goodacre, Elizabeth J. British
            Register of Reading Research, No. 4. Reading:
            Berkshire: University of Reading School of Education,
            1979.

2.C.276.   Bentley, Diana, and Goodacre, Elizabeth J. British
            Register of Reading Research, No. 5. Reading,
            Berkshire: University of Reading School of Education,
            1980.

2.C.277.   Bentley, Diana, and Goodacre, Elizabeth J. British
            Register of Reading Research, No. 6. Reading,
            Berkshire: University of Reading School of Education,
            1981.

2.C.278.   Bentley, Diana, and Goodacre, Elizabeth J. British
            Register of Reading Research, No. 7. Reading,
            Berkshire: University of Reading School of Education,
            1982.

2.C.279.   Bentley, Diana, and Goodacre, Elizabeth J. British
            Register of Reading Research, No. 8. Reading,
            Berkshire: University of Reading School of Education,
            1983.

2.C.280.   Bentley, Diana, and Goodacre, Elizabeth J. British
            Register of Reading Research, No. 9. Reading,
            Berkshire: University of Reading School of Education,
            1984.

2.C.281.   Berg, Leila, ed. Nippers (Five Groups of Graded Books
            for Children Aged 6 to 9). Basingstoke, Hants:
            Macmillan, 1969.

2.C.282.   Bernstein, B. "Language and Social Class." British
            Journal of Sociology 11(1960): 271-276.

2.C.283.   Bernstein, B., and Henderson, D. "Social Class
            Differences in the Relevance of Language to
            Socialization." Sociology 3(1969): 1-20.

2.C.284.   Beswick, R. "Report from England; Learning to Read in a
            Matter of Months." Grade Teacher 88, (September

1970): 59-60.

2.C.285.   Birch, L. B. "Improvement of Reading Ability." British
           Journal of Educational Psychology 20, (June 1950):
           73-76.

2.C.286.   Blake, M. e. "Reading Instruction in England: A
           Qualitative View." The New England Reading
           Association Journal 21, (Winter 1986): 12-18.

2.C.287.   Booth, Vera Southgate. "Structuring Reading Materials for
           Beginning Reading." In Reading: A Human Right and a
           Human Problem, pp. 73-79. Edited by Ralph C. Staiger
           and Oliver Andresen. Newark, Delaware: International
           Reading Association, 1969.

2.C.288.   Breakthrough to Literacy. (Materials include Teacher's
           Manual, Teacher's Sentence Maker, Magnetic Board Kit,
           Children's Sentence Maker and Word Maker, and 24 Read-
           ing Books). Harlow, Essex: Longman, 1970.

2.C.289.   Calnan, M., and Richardson, K. "Speech Problems Among
           Children in a National Survey-Associations with
           Reading, General Ability, Mathematics and Syntactic
           Maturity." Educational Studies 3, 1(March 1977):
           55-66.

2.C.290.   Cashdan, A. "Reflections on the Beginning Reading Program."
           The Reading Teacher 26, (January 1983): 384-388.

2.C.291.   Cashdan, A., et al. "Children Receiving Remedial Teaching
           in Reading." Educational Research 13, (February 1971):
           98-105.

2.C.292.   Cashdan, A., and Pumfrey, P. D. "Some Effects of the
           Remedial Teaching of Reading." Educational Research
           11(1969): 138-142.

2.C.293.   Coolahan, John. "Three Eras of English Reading in Irish
           National Schools." In Studies in Reading, pp. 12-26.
           Edited by Vincent Greaney. Dublin: The Educational
           Company, 1977.

2.C.294.   Corrall, I. "Reading Crash Course." Forum 19, (Spring
           1977): 51-54.

2.C.295.   Cummings, James. See entry 2.A.10.

2.C.296.   Dalgleish, B. W. J., and Enkelmann, Susan. "The
           Interpretation of Pronomial Reference by Retarded and
           Normal Readers." British Journal of Educational
           Psychology 49, 3(November 1979): 290-296.

2.C.297.   Davies, William James Frank. Teaching Reading in Early
           England. New York: Barnes and Noble, 1974.

2.C.298.   Day, B. D., and Swetenburg, J. S. O. "Where Children
            Write to Read." **Childhood Education** 54, (March 1978):
            229-233.

2.C.299.   Department of Education and Science. (British
            Government). **Progress in Reading 1948-1964.**
            Education Pamphlet No. 50. London: Author, 1966.

2.C.300.   Department of Education and Science. **Primary Education
            in Wales.** ("The Gittens Report"). London: H.M.S.O.,
            1968.

2.C.301.   Downing, John. "Reading Readiness Re-examined." In **The
            First International Reading Symposium.** Edited by John
            Downing. London: Cassell, 1966.

2.C.302.   Downing, John. "I.T.A. American versus British
            Experience." **Phi Delta Kappan** 52(March 1971):   416-
            419.

2.C.303.   Downing, John. "I.T.A. and Slow Learners: A
            Reappraisal." In **Reading: Problems and Practices.**
            Edited by J. F. Reid. London: Ward, Lock, 1972.

2.C.304.   Downing, J. "Teaching Reading with I.T.A. in Britain."
            Phi Delta Kappan 45, (April 1964): 322-329.

2.C.305.   Downing, John. "Language Arts in the British Primary
            School Revolution." In **Proceedings of the NCTE
            Language Arts Conference,** St. Louis, March 5-7, 1970.
            Champaign, Illinois: National Council of Teachers of
            English, 1972.

2.C.306.   Featherstone, J., and Cohen, D. K. "Children and Their
            Primary Schools: Plowden Report." **Harvard
            Educational Review** 38(Spring 1968):   317-340.

2.C.307.   Feeley, Joan T. "Reading with T.V.": British and
            American Approaches." **The Reading Teacher** 30, 3
            (December 1976):   271-275.

2.C.308.   Foselman, Ken, et al. "Ability-Grouping in Secondary
            Schools and Attainment." **Educational Studies** 4, 3
            (October 1978):   201-212.

2.C.309.   Gattegno, C. **Words in Color: Background and Principles.**
            Chicago: Learning Materials, Inc., 1962.

2.C.310.   Gessert, Beth. "Specific Reading Difficulties in Great
            Britain." In **Reading Disabilities: an International
            Perspective,** pp. 193-208. Edited by Lester Tarnopol
            and Muriel Tarnopol. Baltimore, Maryland: University
            Park Press, 1976.

2.C.311.   Godfrey, P. "Reading: An Individual Approach." **Forum**
            24, (Spring 1982):   43-44.

2.C.312.   Gooch, S. "Four Years On." **New Society** 193(1966): 10-12.

2.C.313.   Goodacre, E. J. **Reading in Infant Classes.** Slough: National Foundation for Educational Research in England and Wales, 1967.

2.C.314.   Goodacre, E. J. "Learning How to Teach Reading- A Research Note on the Findings of a Postal Survey." In **Conference: Professional Preparation of Students For the Teaching of Reading.** Edited by M. Peters. Cambridge: Cambridge Institute of Education, 1969.

2.C.315.   Goodacre, E. J. "Published Reading Schemes." **Educational Research** 12(1969): 30-35.

2.C.316.   Goodacre, Elizabeth J. "Great Britain." In **Comparative Reading,** pp. 360-382. Edited by John Downing. New York: Macmillan, 1973.

2.C.317.   Goodacre, Elizabeth J. "Reading Research in Britain-- 1977." **Reading** 12, (April 1978): 6-14.

2.C.318.   Goodacre, Elizabeth J. "Reading Research in Great Britain--1978." **Reading** 13, (April 1979): 4-12.

2.C.319.   Goodacre, Elizabeth J. "Reading Research in Great Britain--1979." **Reading** 14, (December 1980): 3-11.

2.C.320.   Goodacre, Elizabeth J. "Reading Research in Great Britain--1980." **Reading** 15, (1981): 5-14.

2.C.321.   Goodacre, Elizabeth J. "Reading Research in Great Britain--1981." **Reading** 16, (1982): 67-78.

2.C.322.   Goodacre, Elizabeth J. "Reading Research in Great Britain--1982." **Reading** 17 (December 1983): 139-146.

2.C.323.   Goodacre, Elizabeth J. "Reading Research in Great Britain--1983." **Reading** 18 (December 1984): 135-144.

2.C.324.   Goodacre, Elizabeth J., and Clark, Margaret, M. "Initial Approaches to Teaching Reading in Scottish and English Schools." **Reading** 5, 2(June 1971): 15-21.

2.C.325.   Gorman, T. P., et al. **Language Performance in Schools.** Primary Survey Report No. 1. London: H.M.S.O., 1982.

2.C.326.   Gorman, T. P., et al. **Language Performance in Schools.** Primary Survey Report No. 2. London: H.M.S.O., 1982.

2.C.327.   Gorman, T. P. et al. **Language Performance in Schools.** Primary Survey Report No. 1. London: H.M.S.O., 1981.

2.C.328.   Great Britain. Standards of Reading, 1948 to 1956.
            London: H.M.S.O., 1957.

2.C.329.   Great Britain. Progress in Reading: 1948-1964. London:
            H.M.S.O., 1966.

2.C.330.   Great Britain. School Council. Research and Development
            Project in Compensatory Education. Aspects of Early
            Reading Growth: A Longitudinal Study. Oxford:
            Blackwell, 1974.

2.C.331.   Green, Frank. "Language Arts Instruction: Lessons from
            the British." Language Arts 63, 4(March 1986): 378-
            382.

2.C.332.   Groebel, Lillian. "A Comparison of Two Strategies in
            Teaching of Reading Comprehension." English Language
            Teaching Journal 33, 4(July 1979): 306-309.

2.C.333.   Hall, Nigel. "Characters in British Basal Series Don't
            Read Either." The Reading Teacher 37, (October 1983):
            22-25.

2.C.334.   Hammond, Dorothy. "Reading Attainment in the Primary
            Schools of Brighton." Educational Research 10(1967):
            57-64.

2.C.335.   Harrison, Colin. "Readability in the United Kingdom."
            Journal of Reading 29, 6(March 1986): 521-529.

2.C.336.   Harrison, Colin. "The Textbook as an Endangered Species:
            the Implications of Economic Decline and Technological
            Advance on the Place of Reading in Learning." Oxford
            Review of Education 7, 3(1981): 231-240.

2.C.337.   Harrop, A., and McCann, C. "Behavior Modification and
            Reading Attainment in the Comprehensive School."
            Educational Research 25, (November 1983): 191-195.

2.C.338.   Harvey, T. J., and Cooper, C. J. "An Investigation into
            Some Possible Factors Affecting Children's Under-
            standing of the Concept of an Electrical Current in
            the Age Range 8-11 Years Old." Educational Studies
            4, 2(June 1978): 149-155.

2.C.339.   Hillman, H. H., and Snowdon, R. L. "Part-Time Classes for
            Young Backward Readers." British Journal of
            Educational Psychology 30, (June 1960): 168-172.

2.C.340.   Horner, Peter. "The Teaching of Reading in England Up to
            1870." Reading 7, 3(December 1973): 3-10.

2.C.341.   Hudson, Jean. "Reading Comprehension in Great Britain."
            Reading Improvement 10(Spring 1973): 4.

2.C.342.   Hughes, Theone. What the British Tell the U.S. About

Writing and Reading. Paper presented at the Annual Great Lakes Regional Conference of the International Reading Conference. Cincinnati: n.p., 1978. ED 175 020.

2.C.343.   Hunter-Grundin, Elizabeth, and Grundin, Hans U., eds. Reading: Implementing the Bullock Report. London: United Kingdom Reading Association, Ward Lock Educational, 1978.

2.C.344.   Ingham, Jennie. Books and Reading Development: The Bradford Book Flood Experiment. London: Heinemann Educational Books, 1981.

2.C.345.   Inner London Education Authority. Literacy Survey: Summary of Interim Results of the Study of Pupils' Reading Standards. London: Inner London Education Authority, 1969.

2.C.346.   Irvine, D. G. The Reading Ability of School-Leavers: A Study of the Extent of Reading Difficulties Among School-Leavers in Liverpool. Liverpool: University of Liverpool, Institute of Extension Studies, 1976.

2.C.347.   Johns, E. "The Age Factor in Reading Retardation." Researchers and Studies (University of Leeds Institute of Education) 24(1962): 1-7.

2.C.348.   Johnson, Terry D. "A Comparison of British and American Reading Instruction." Phi Delta Kappan 55, 10(June 1974): 678-679.

2.C.349.   Jones, J. K. Colour Story Reading: A Research Report. London: Nelson, 1967.

2.C.350.   Jones, J. K. "A Research Report on Colour Story Reading." Journal of Typographic Research 2(January 1968): 53-58.

2.C.351.   Lee, W. R. Spelling Irregularity and Reading Difficulty in English. London: NFER in England and Wales, 1960.

2.C.352.   Lobban, G. "Presentation of Sex-Roles in British Reading Schemes." Forum 16, (Spring 1974): 57-60.

2.C.353.   Lovell, K. et al. "Summary of a Study of the Reading Ages of Children Who Had Been Given Remedial Teaching." British Journal of Educational Psychology 32, (February 1962): 66-71.

2.C.354.   Lovell, K., et al. "Further Study of the Educational Progress of Children Who had Received Remedial Education." British Journal of Educational Psychology 33, (February 1963): 3-9.

2.C.355.   Mabey, Christine. "Black British Literacy: A Study of

Reading Attainment of London Black Children from 8 to 15 Years." Educational Research 23, 8(February 1981): 83-95.

2.C.356.   Merritt, J. E. "Recent Developments in Great Britain."
            Journal of Reading 17, (February 1974): 367-372.

2.C.357.   Ministry of Education. Reading Ability: Some Suggestions
            for Helping the Backward. Pamphlet No. 18. London:
            H.M.S.O., 1950.

2.C.358.   Morris, J. M. Reading in the Primary School. London:
            Newnes, 1959.

2.C.359.   Morris, J. M. "Teaching of Reading to Beginners in the
            United Kingdom." Canadian Education and Research
            Digest 3, (March 1963): 10-16.

2.C.360.   Morris, Joyce. Standards and Progress in Reading.
            Slough: NFER in England and Wales, 1966.

2.C.361.   Morris, Joyce. "Beginning Reading in England." In
            Reading: A Human Right and a Human Problem, pp. 23-
            28. Edited by Ralph C. Staiger and Oliver Andresen.
            Newark, Delaware: International Reading Association,
            1969.

2.C.362.   Moyle, Donald. "British Trends in Teacher Education in
            Reading." Australian Journal of Reading 2, 1(March
            1979): 18-21.

2.C.363.   Mycock, M. "A Comparison of Vertical Grouping and
            Horizontal Grouping in the Infant School." British
            Journal of Educational Psychology 37(1967): 133-135.

2.C.364.   Neville, M. H., and Pugh, A. K. "Context in Reading and
            Listening: Variations in Approach to Cloze Tasks."
            Reading Research Quarterly 12, 1(76-77): 13-31.

2.C.365.   Newman, G. R. "Angry Child Learns to Read." Grade Teacher
            87, (February 1970): 95-96.

2.C.366.   Peaker, Gilbert F. "The Aims and Achievements of English
            Primary Education." International Review of Education
            17, 4(1971): 442-456.

2.C.367.   Peterson, Raymond P. "A Comparison of the Reading and
            Spelling Achievements of Groups of English and
            American Children." Doctoral Dissertation, University
            of Michigan, Ann Arbor, 1964.

2.C.368.   Philip, J. L., and Goyen, J. "Innovation in Reading in
            Britain." Paris: UNESCO, 1973.

2.C.369.   Pidgeon, D. A. "School Type Differences in Ability and
            Attainment." Educational Research 1(1959): 62-71.

2.C.370.   Pidgeon, D. A. Expectation and Pupil Performance. Slough:
            NFER, 1970.

2.C.371.   Pollard, Barbara. "Teaching English, The English Way."
            English Journal 58, 4(April 1969): 586-590.

2.C.372.   Pumfrey, Peter D. "The Reading Attainments of British
            Children of Parents of West Indian Origins: Challenge
            and Response." Reading 17 (July 1983): 111-124.

2.C.373.   Push, A. K. "Training in Children's Literature--
            Children's Literature in Great Britain: Courses and
            Emphases." Bookbind 10, 2(1972): 35-38.

2.C.374.   Russell, D. R. "Primary Reading Programs in England and
            Scotland." Elementary School Journal 57(May 1957):
            446-451.

2.C.375.   Sanderson, A. E. "The Idea of Reading Readiness: A Re-
            examination." Educational Research 6(1963): 3-9.

2.C.376.   Schofer, Gil. "Reading Preferences of British and
            American Elementary Children." Reading Improvement
            18, 2(Summer 1981): 127-131.

2.C.377.   Scholl, Geraldine T. "The Reading and Spelling
            Achievement of a Group of English Children as Judged
            by the Standards of an American Achievement Test."
            Doctoral dissertation. University of Michigan, Ann
            Arbor, 1960.

2.C.378.   Scottish Council for Research in Education. Educational
            Research in the United Kingdom: Scotland 1970-1972.
            Edinburgh: Scottish Education Department, 1975.
            ED 113 285.

2.C.379.   Shafer, Robert E. A Comparative Study of Successful
            Practices and Materials for Teaching Reading in the
            Primary Schools as Viewed by Teachers in England and
            the United States. Paper presented at the Annual
            Meeting of the United Kingdom Reading Association.
            Durham, England: n.p., 1976. ED 145 364.

2.C.380.   Shafer, Robert E., and Shafer, Susanne, M. "Teacher
            Attitudes Towards Children's Language in West Germany
            and England." In Reading: What of the Future? pp.
            249-260. Edited by Donald Moyle. London: United
            Kingdom Reading Association, 1975.

2.C.381.   Shearer, E. "The Effect of Date of Birth on Teachers'
            Assessments of Children." Educational Research 10
            (1967): 51-56.

2.C.382.   Shields, M. "Reading and Transition to Junior School."
            Educational Research 11(1968): 143-147.

2.C.383.   Southgate, V. "Approaching I.T.A. Results with Caution."
            Educational Research 7(1965):   83-96.

2.C.384.   Southgate, V. "Identifying Major Problems in Reading in
            England." International Reading Association Con-
            ference Proceedings 13, Part 1. 1969, 863-870.

2.C.385.   Southgate, V., and Roberts, G. R. **Reading--Which**
            Approach? London: University of London Press, 1970.

2.C.386.   Spitzer, Rosina. "Why Johnny Can Read." **Clearing House**
            51, 5(January 1978):   234-239.

2.C.387.   Start, K. B., and Wells, B. K. **The Trend of Reading**
            Standards. National Foundation for Educational
            Research in England and Wales, 1972.

2.C.388.   "Two Years Behind in Reading; Gap in Reading Comprehension
            Between British and Dublin Children." **Times**
            Educational Supplement 2860: 7, March 13, 1970.

2.C.389.   Weber, Lillian. **The English Infant School and Informal**
            Education. Englewood Cliffs, New Jersey: Prentice-
            Hall, 1971. ED 057 593.

2.C.390.   Wiseman, S. **Education and Environment.** Manchester:
            Manchester University Press, 1964.

2.C.391.   Wright, Esmond, comp. **The Special Relationship: The**
            United States as the British Have Seen It. A
            Selective Reading List by British Writers. London:
            National Book League, 1976. ED 142 460.

        18. Ethiopia

2.C.392.   Starr, Dartha Fay, and Starr, Fay H. "Learning to Read in
            Ethiopia." Journal of Reading 21, 6(March 1978).

        19. Fiji

2.C.393.   Elley, W. B., and Mangubhai, F. "The Impact of Reading on
            Second Language Learning." **Reading Research Quarterly**
            19, (Fall 1983):   53-67.

        20. Finland

2.C.394.   Arajarvi, T.; Louhivouri, K; Hagman, H.; Syvalahti, R.;
            and Hietanen, A. "The Role of Specific Reading and
            Writing Difficulties in Various School Problems."
            Annales Paediatriae Fenniae 11(1965): 138.

2.C.395.   Arajarvi, T.; Syvalahti, R.; and Hagman, H. "On the
            Specific Reading and Writing Difficulties of

Children." Psychiatria Fennica, pp. 185-190.

2.C.396.   Karvonen, J. The Enrichment of Vocabulary and the Basic
            Skills of Verbal Communication. Jyvaskyla, Finland:
            Jyvaskyla Studies in Education, University of
            Jyvaskyla, 1970.

2.C.397.   Kyostio, O. K. "Reading Levels Among 15-Year-Old Boys and
            Girls." Kasvatus ja Koulu 6(1962): 289-315.

2.C.398.   Kyostio. O. K. "Finland." In Comparative Reading, pp.
            308-318. Edited by John Downing. New York:
            Macmillan, 1973.

2.C.399.   Kyostio, O. K. "Development of Reading Skill During
            Elementary School in Finland." The Reading Teacher
            35, 5(February 1980): 519-526.

2.C.400.   Kyostio, O. K., and Vaherva, T. "Reading and Forgetting
            Among Young Children." Scandanavian Journal of
            Educational Research 3(1969): 129-146.

2.C.401.   Lehtovaara, A., and Saarinen, P. School Age Reading
            Interests. Helsinki: Finnish Academy of Science,
            1964.

2.C.402.   Neville, Mary H. "Reading in the First School: A
            Comparison with Finland." Reading 6, 3(December
            1972): 18-22.

2.C.403.   Ranta, T. M. "Method and Materials of Teaching Reading in
            Finland Under Church and State." Doctoral
            dissertation. University of Minnesota, 1964.

2.C.404.   Rauhala, Ritva A. I. "Reading Teacher as Cooperator--
            Finland." The Reading Teacher 35, 4(January 1982):
            412-417.

2.C.405.   Somerkivi, Urho. Lukutaito Ja Sen Opettaminen Ala-
            asteilla. Helsinki: Otava, 1958.

2.C.405.   Syvalahti, Raija. "Reading-Writing Disabilities in
            Finland." In Reading Disabilities: An International
            Perspective, pp. 175-178. Edited by Lester Tarnopol
            and Muriel Tarnopol. Baltimore, Maryland: University
            Park Press, 1976.

2.C.407.   Venezky, Richard L. The Letter-Sound Generalizations of
            First, Second and Third Grade Finnish Children.
            Madison, Wisconsin: Wisconsin Research and
            Development Center for Cognitive Learning, 1972.

2.C.408.   Viitaniemi, Eero. Kansakoulun Neljasluok- Kalaisten
            Lukutaidon Rakenteesta Ja Arvostelusta. Turku:
            University of Turku, 1964.

2.C.409.   Viitaniemi, Eero. "Has There Been a Decline in Reading
             Ability Among Pupils of Finnish 'Comprehensive'
             Schools." Scandanavian Journal of Educational
             Research 27, 4(1983): 181-200.

2.C.410.   Vikainen (Laurinen). Inkeri Lausetajun Kehityksesta.
             Helsinki: University of Helsinki, 1955.

2.C.411.   Vikainen (Laurinen). Inkeri, A Diagnosis of Specific
             Backwardness in Spelling. Turku: University of
             Turku, 1965.

2.C.412.   Ylisto, I. P. "Early Reading Responses of Young Finnish
             Children." The Reading Teacher 31, (November 1977):
             167-172.

        21. France

2.C.413.   Bloomfield, Leonard. "Linguistics and Reading."
             Elementary English Review 19(1942): 125-130.

2.C.414.   Bouygues, C. "Civilisation- Culture Ou Apprentissage
             D'une Lecture (Civilization- Culture or Reading
             Exercise)." French Review 44, 1(October 1970): 51-62.

2.C.415.   Chanson, M., and Olanie, S. Lecture Globale-Lecture
             Active. Paris: Librairie Centrale d'Education
             Nouvelle, 1949, p. 37.

2.C.416.   Chiland, Colette. "The Teaching of Reading in France."
             In The Second International Reading Symposium, pp.
             35-70. Edited by John Downing and Amy Brown. London:
             Cassell, 1967.

2.C.417.   Dupart, Annie. "Kindergarten Teachers--Members of a
             Reading Research Lab in France: An Interview with
             Alain Bentolila." The Reading Teacher 38, 7(March
             1985): 654-657.

2.C.418.   Fraser, W. R. Reforms and Restraints in Modern French
             Education. London: Routledge and Kegan Paul, 1971.

2.C.419.   International Education Yearbook. Geneva: International
             Bureau of Education, 1959.

2.C.420.   Kandel, I. L. French Elementary Schools. New York:
             Teachers College, Columbia University, 1926.

2.C.421.   Lobrot, Michel G. "Remedial Education in France." In
             Reading: Current Research and Practice, pp. 112-117.
             Edited by Amy L. Brown. Edinburgh: Chambers, 1967.

2.C.422.   Manuals for Primary Education. Geneva: International
             Bureau of Education, 1959.

2.C.423.   Perrot, Colette. "Difficultes De Lecture En Sixieme Et
            Cinquieme." Cahiers Pedagogiques 13(March 1958):
            32-33.

2.C.424.   Piacere, Andree. "Integration Vitesse-Precision A Une
            Epreuve De Barrage De Signes Chez Les Enfants Mauvais
            Lecteurs." In Reading: A Human Right and a Human
            Problem, pp. 156-166. Edited by Ralph C. Staiger and
            Oliver Andresen. Newark, Delaware: International
            Reading Association, 1969.

2.C.425.   Richaudeau, Francois. "Some French Works on Prose Read-
            ability and Syntax." Journal of Reading 24, 6
            (March 1981): 503-508.

2.C.426.   Ruthman, Paul E. "France." In Comparative Reading, pp.
            319-341. Edited by John Downing. New York:
            Macmillan, 1973.

2.C.427.   Ruthman, Paul E. "Utilizing Available Published Data:
            The Teaching of Reading in the Elementary Schools of
            France." In Reading: What of the Future? pp. 279-
            285. Edited by Donald Moyle. London: United Kingdom
            Reading Association, 1975.

2.C.428.   Valdman, A., et al. A Drillbook of French Pronunciation.
            New York: Harper, 1964.

2.C.429.   Zazzo, Rene. "Conclusion De Notre Enquete Sur
            L'Apprentissage De La Lecture." L'Ecole Et La Nation
            60(July 1959): 7-8.

22. Germany, East

2.C.430.   Council on International Books for Children, Inc. "The
            Five Chinese Brothers: Time to Retire; Exit Goblins
            and Fairies: Enter a New Children's Theatre; What
            Children are Reading in GDR Schools." Interracial
            Books for Children Bulletin 8, 3(1977): L1977.
            ED 145 018.

2.C.431.   Kienitz, W. "On the Marxist Approach to Comparative
            Education in the German Democratic Republic."
            Comparative Education 7(August 1971): 21-31.

2.C.432.   Raynor, Phyllis F. "Development of Programs for Children
            with Specific Reading Disabilities in the German
            Democratic Republic." The Reading Teacher 39, 9(May
            1986): 912-918.

2.C.433.   Slepack, Donna Grund. A Comparative Study of Sex Role
            Stereotyping in GDR (German Democratic Republic) and
            USA Children's Readers. Paper presented at the
            International Studies Association Conference. St.
            Louis: n.p., 1977. ED 165 189.

23. Germany, West

2.C.434.   "The Alphabetic Principle in Hebrew and German Contrasted
            to the Alphabetic Principle in English." Highlights
            of the International Reading Association 1965 Pre-
            Convention Institute, Linguistics and Reading.
            Newark, Delaware: International Reading Association,
            1966, pp. 44-50.

2.C.435.   Archer, Julie, et al. Umweltverschmutzung. German Ecology
            Packet: Resource Units and Materials for German
            Classes at all Levels. St. Paul: Minnesota State
            Department of Education, Division of Instruction,
            1972. ED 060 696.

2.C.436.   Biglmaier, Franz. Lesestorungen-Diagnose und Behandlung.
            Munich and Basel: Ernest Reinhard Verlag, 1968.

2.C.437.   Biglmaier, Franz. "Informelle Lehrertests Im
            Rechtschreigunterricht- Fehleranalyse und
            Fehlerbehandlung." Die Grundschule 2(April 1970).

2.C.438.   Biglmaier, Franz. "Germany." In Comparative Reading, pp.
            342-359. Edited by John Downing. Macmillan, 1973.

2.C.439.   Block, Robert. "Das Kind und Die Schule." In Deutsche
            Sprachstatistik. Edited by Meier Helmut. Hildesheim:
            Georg Olms Verlagsbuchhandlung, 1967.

2.C.440.   Bodenman, Paul S. The Educational System of the Federal
            Republic of Germany. Washington, D.C.: Office of
            Education (DHEW), Report No.- OE-76-19127. 1976.
            ED 151 265.

2.C.441.   Bosch, B. Grundlagen Des Erstleseunterrichts. 2nd
            Edition. Angermund: 1949.

2.C.442.   Brugelman,, H. J. "Discovering Print: A Process Approach
            to Initial Reading and Writing in West Germany." The
            Reading Teacher 40, (December 1986): 294-298.

2.C.443.   Erdmann, B., and Dodge, R. Psychologische Untersuchungen
            Uber Das Lesen Auf Experimenteller Grundlage. Halle:
            Niemeyer, 1898.

2.C.444.   Frey, H. "Improving the Performance of Poor Readers
            Through Autogenic Relaxation Training." The Reading
            Teacher 33, (May 1980): 928-932.

2.C.445.   Hartmann, W. Vergleichende Untersuchungen Zum
            Ganzheitsverfahren Vom 1 Bis 4 Schuljahr. Leipzig:
            n.p., 1941.

2.C.446.   Hasler, Herbert and Schwartz, Erwin. "Lehrer Und
            Lesemethoden." Westermanns Padagogische Beitrage
            4(1966).

2.C.447.   Hoffmann, J. "Experimentell-psychologische Untersuchungen
            Uber Leseleistungen Von Schulkindern." **Archiv Fur
            Die Gesamte Psychologie** (1927).

2.C.448.   Jantzen, J. M. "Teaching Reading in West Germany."
            Elementary English 41, (October 1964): 640-642.

2.C.449.   Kainz, Friedrich. **Psychologie Der Sprache**, Vol. IV:
            Speziette Sprachpsychologie. Stuttgart: Ferdinand
            Enke Verlag, 1956.

2.C.450.   Katzenberger, L. F. "Schulanganger Und Lesenlernen. Eine
            Kritische Uberprufung Der Untersuchungsbefunde Von
            Bosch Uber Die Fahigkeit Des Schulneulinges Zur
            Sprachvergegenstandlichung Und Sprachanalyse." Schule
            Und Psychologie 11, 14(1967): 345-359.

2.C.451.   Kern, Artur, and Kern, Erwin. **Lesen Und Lesenlernen.**
            Freiburg: Verlag herden, 1956.

2.C.452.   Kirchhoff, Hans. **Verbale Lese-und Rechtschreibschwache Im
            Kindersalter**, 3rd Edition. Basel: S. Karger, 1964.

2.C.453.   Klasen, Edith. "Learning Disabilities: The German
            Perspective." In **Reading Disabilities:: An Inter-
            national Perspective**, pp. 179-191. Edited by Lester
            Tarnopol and Muriel Tarnopol. Baltimore, Maryland:
            University Park Press, 1976.

2.C.454.   Korte, W. "Uber Die Gestaltauffassung Im Indirekten
            Sehen." **Zeitschrift Fur Psychologie** (1923).

2.C.455.   Linder, Maria. "Uber Legasthenie (spez. Leseschwache)."
            Zeitschrift Fur Kinderpsychiatrie 18(1951).

2.C.456.   Messmer, O. "Zur Psychologie Des Lesens Bei Kindern Und
            Erwachsenen." **Archiv Fur Die Gesamte Psychologie**,
            II (1904).

2.C.457.   Muller, H. **Methoden Des Erstleseunterrichts Und Ihre
            Ergebnisse.** Meisenheim Am Glan: Hain, 1964.

2.C.458.   Pfaffenberger, H. **Untersuchungen Uber Die Visuelle
            Gestaltwahrnehmung Vorschulpflichtiger Kinder.**
            Weinheim: Beltz Verlag, 1960, 1967.

2.C.459.   Preston, R. C. "Issues Raise by the Wiesbaden-
            Philadelphia Reading Study." **Comparative Education
            Review** 7(June 1963): 61-65.

2.C.460.   Preston, R. C. "Comparison of Word-Recognition Skill in
            German and in American Children." **Elementary School
            Journal** 53, (April 1953): 443-446.

2.C.461.   Pribic, Rado. "Young People's Literature in the Federal
            Republic of Germany Today." **Journal of Reading** 24,

4(January 1981):   304-307.

2.C.462.   Ranschburg, P. Die Leseschwache (Legasthenie) Und
             Rechenschwache (Arithmathenie) Der Schulkinder Im
             Lichte Des Experiments. Berlin: Springer, 1916.

2.C.463.   Reinhard, Ludwig. "Fibelfruhling!- Fibelsegen? Eine
             Kritische Sichtung Der Leselernbucher Fur Die Zeit
             1945-1958." Die Scholle 12(1958).

2.C.464.   Reinhard, Ludwig. Im Wundergarten, Fibel In 3 Teilen Fur
             Volksschulen, 1st ed. Munich: Bayerischer Schulbuch-
             Verlag, 1951; 7th rev. ed., 1967.

2.C.465.   Reinhard, Ludwig. Schreiben Macht Spass. Eine Schreib-
             fibel Fur Volksschulen. Munich: Bayerischer
             Schulbuch-Verlag, 1965.

2.C.466.   Robinson, H. M. "Reading in Germany and at Home."
             Elementary School Journal 62(May 1962):   409.

2.C.467.   Sander, F. Experimentelle Ergebnisse Der
             Gestaltpsychologie, Uber Die Sinnerfullung Optischer
             Komplexe Bei Schwachsinnigen, Bericht Des 4.
             Kongresses Fur Heilpadagogik, 1929.

2.C.468.   Schenk-Danzinger, Lotte. "Probleme Der Legasthenie."
             Schweizerische Zeitschrift Fur Psychologie 20(1961):
             29-48.

2.C.469.   Schenk-Danzinger, Lotte. Handbuch Der Legasthenie Im
             Kindersalter. Weinheim: Beltz, 1968.

2.C.470.   Schwartz, R., and Allington, R. L. "Comparison of
             American and West German Basal Texts." The Reading
             Teacher 31(December 1977): 280-282.

2.C.471.   Shafer, Robert E., et al. See Section 2.C.17 entry no. 380.

2.C.472.   Straub, W. "Versagt Die Ganzheitsmethode? Oder Lernen
             Ganzheitlich Unterrichtete Kinder Schlechter Lesen Als
             Synthetisch Unterrichtete Kinder?" Die
             Ganzheitsschule 9(1960).

2.C.473.   Valtin, Renate. "German Studies of Dyslexia:
             Implications for Education." Journal of Research in
             Reading 7, 2(September 1984):   79-102.

2.C.474.   Zeitler, Julius. "Tachistoskopische Untersuchungen Uber
             Da Lesen." Philosophische Studien 16(1900):   380-463.

24.   Ghana

2.C.475.   Katei, S. I. A. Reading Habits of Ghanaians. N.P.,
             [1979].

25. Greece

2.C.476.   Mavrogenes, Nancy A. "Reading in Ancient Greece."
              Journal of Reading 23, 8(May 1980): 691-697.

2.C.477.   Mavrogenese, Nancy. "Cultural Effects on Teaching Reading
              in Modern Greece." Journal of Reading 26, 7(April
              1983): 622-628.

2.C.478.   Sikiotis, N. "Reading Habits and Preferences of Secondary
              School Pupils in Greece." English Language Teaching
              Journal 35, (April 1981): 300-306.

2.C.479.   Ungaro, Daniel. "The Twain Do Meet." Elementary English
              49, 5(May 1972): 717-720.

26. Guatemala

2.C.480.   Lasky, Beth. Training Teachers at a School for the Handi-
              capped in Quezaltenanso, Guatemala. Paper presented
              at the Council for Exceptional Children Conference on
              the Exceptional Bilingual Child. New Orleans: n.p.,
              1981. ED 210 856.

2.C.481.   Salisbury, D. F., and Hilton, T. S. E. "Exploring
              Potential Application of the Structured Tutoring Model
              to Teaching Reading in Guatemala." International
              Journal of Instructional Media 11, 4(1983/1984): 361-
              367.

27. Haiti

2.C.482.   McConnell, H. O. "Teaching Them to Read: Literacy
              Campaign in Haiti." International Review of Missions
              42, (October 1953): 438-445.

28. Hong Kong

2.C.483.   Chuang, Chai-hsuan. A Fundamental Vocabulary of Chinese
              Characters. China: China Press, 1938 (in Chinese).

2.C.484.   de Francis, John. Nationalism and Language Reform in
              China. Princeton, New Jersey: Princeton University
              Press, 1950.

2.C.485.   Downey, T. J. "English or Chinese? The Medium of
              Instruction in Hong Kong." Compare 7(April 1977):
              67-72.

2.C.486.   Herdan, Gustav. Language as Choice and Chance.
              Groningen, Holland: P. Noorhoff, 1956.

2.C.487.   Herdan, Gustav. The Calculus of Linguistic Observations.
            The Hague: Mouton, 1962.

2.C.488.   Herdan, Gustav. The Structuralist Approach to Chinese
            Grammar and Vocabulary. The Hague: Mounton, 1964.

2.C.489.   Kennedy, George A. "Monosyllabic Myth." Journal of the
            American Oriental Society 71, 3(1951).

2.C.490.   Kennedy, George A. The Minimum Vocabularies of Written
            Chinese. New Haven, Connecticut: Yale University
            Press, 1954.

2.C.491.   Kline, Carl L., and Lee, Norma. "A Transcultural Study of
            Dyslexia: Analysis of Reading Disabilities in 425
            Chinese Children Simultaneously Learning to Read and
            Write in English and in Chinese." Bulletin of the
            Orton Society 19(1969): 67-81.

2.C.492.   Leong, C. K. An Experimental Study of the Vocabulary of
            Written Chinese Among Primary III Children in Hong
            Kong. Paper presented at the Fifteenth Annual
            Convention of the International Reading Association.
            Anaheim, California: n.p., 1970.

2.C.493.   Leong, C. K. Vocabulary of Written Chinese: Contemporary
            Usage Among Junior III Children in Hong Kong. Hong
            Kong: Government Printer, 1968.

2.C.494.   Leong, Che Kan. "Hong Kong." In Comparative Reading,
            pp. 383-402. Edited by John Downing. New York:
            Macmillan, 1973.

2.C.495.   Report of the Working Party on the Teaching of Chinese.
            Hong Kong: Government Printer, 1968.

2.C.496.   Schwedel, Allan M. "Must We Use Phonology to Read? What
            Chinese Can Tell Us." Journal of Reading 26, 8(May
            1983): 707-713.

29. Hungary

2.C.497.   Horvath, A., and Andor, M. "Representation of Social
            Reading in the Elementary School Reading--Books."
            International Journal of Political Education 5, 4
            (December 1982): 355-376.

2.C.498.   Illes, Sandor, and Meixner, Ildikoi. "Learning and
            Reading Disabilities in Hungary." In Reading
            Disabilities: An International Perspective, pp. 209-
            226. Edited by Lester Tarnopol and Muriel Tarnopol.
            Baltimore, Maryland: University Park Press, 1976.

2.C.499.   Kamavas, Istvan, and Nagy, Attila. "Reading Research in
           Hungary." Journal of Research in Reading 4,
           2(September 1981): 81-91.

     30.   India

2.C.500.   Hastings, Dorothy M. H. Effects of Self-Contained, Inde-
           pendent Learning Plan and Integrated Education
           Programs on Achievement in Reading and Math for
           Punjabi-English K-3 Bilingual Students. Ann Arbor,
           Michigan: Dissertation Abstracts, V42(05), Sec. A,
           p. 2012, 1981.

2.C.501.   Lakdawala, V. T. Gujarati Vocabulary of Children Between
           6 and 10 Years. Bombay: University of Bombay, 1951.

2.C.502.   Lakdawala, V. T. The Basic Vocabulary of Gujarati
           Children at the Age of 13 Plus. Bombay: University
           of Bombay, 1960.

2.C.503.   Mehrotra, Preet Vanti. "Issues in Developing Materials
           for Beginning Reading in Hindi." In Mother Tongue
           or Second Language. Edited by Dina Feitelson.
           Newark, Delaware: International Reading Association,
           1979.

2.C.504.   Oommen, Chinna (nee Chacko). "India." In Comparative
           Reading, pp. 403-425. Edited by John Downing. New
           York: Macmillan, 1973.

2.C.505.   Prakash, Ved. "Stagnation and Wastage." In Indian
           Yearbook of Education. New Delhi: NCERT, 1965.

2.C.506.   Rawal, R. T. The Basic Vocabulary of Gujarati Children at
           the Age of 12 Plus. Bombay: University of Bombay,
           1959.

2.C.507.   Rawat, D. S. A Battery of Reading Readiness Tests. New
           Delhi: NCERT, 1964.

2.C.508.   Reading Project. A Classified Bibliography of Research
           Studies on Reading Conducted at Indian Universities.
           New Delhi: NCERT, 1963.

2.C.509.   Reading Project. Teaching Reading: A Challenge. New
           Delhi: NCERT, 1966.

2.C.510.   Srinivasachari, G. "Selection of Words and Structures for
           Readers." In Reading: A Human Right and a Human
           Problem, pp. 80-86. Edited by Ralph C. Staiger and
           Oliver Andresen. Newark, Delaware: International
           Reading Association, 1969.

2.C.511.   Vakil, K. S.The Basic Vocabulary of Gujarati Children at
             the Age of 11 Plus. Bombay: University of Bombay,
             1955.

     31. Iran

2.C.512.   Deckert, Glenn D. "Sociological Barriers to the Reading
             Habit: The Case of Iran." Journal of Reading 25, 8
             (May 1982): 742-749.

2.C.513.   The Educational System of Iran. Washington, D.C.:
             Institute of International Studies (DHEW/OE), Report
             No. - DHEW- OE-75-19114. ED 104 741.

2.C.514.   Edwards, T. J. "Teaching of Reading in Iran." The Read-
             ing Teacher 16, (September 1962): 7-12.

2.C.515.   International Institute for Adult Literary Methods.
             Programme Unit. A Survey of Reader Interest and
             Preference in Eight Iranian Villages. Tehran: IIALM,
             1977.

2.C.516.   Rahimi, Nassar. "Case Study: Iran." In A Reason to
             Read: A Report on an International Symposium on the
             Promotion of the Reading Habit, pp. 41-44. New York
             Academy for Educational Development and UNESCO, 1976.

     32. Ireland

2.C.517.   Coolahan, John. See Section 2.C.17 entry no. 293.

2.C.518.   Cummings, James. See Section 2.A. entry no. 10.

2.C.519.   Downing, John. See Section 2.A. entry no. 14.

2.C.520.   Fontes, P. J.; Kellaghan, T.; and O'Brien, M. "Relation-
             ships Between Time Spent Teaching Classroom
             Organization, and Reading Achievement." Irish Journal
             of Education 15, 1&2(Summer & Winter 1981): 79-91.

2.C.521.   Greaney, Vincent. "Trends in Attainment in Irish From
             1973 to 1977." The Irish Journal of Education
             12(Summer/Winter 1978): 22-35.

2.C.522.   Greaney, Vincent. "Review of Reading Research in the
             Republic of Ireland." In Studies in Reading.
             Edited by Vincent Greaney. Dublin: The Educational
             Company, 1977.

2.C.523.   Greaney, Vincent, and Kelly, Paul. "Reading Standards in
             Irish Post-Primary Schools." In Studies in Reading,
             pp. 44-56. Edited by Vincent Greaney. Dublin: The
             Educational Company, 1977.

2.C.524.   Harden, Harold D. **Education in Ireland.** Pensacola,
            Florida: University of West Florida, Department of
            Admissions; Educational Research and Development
            Center, 1976. ED 142 471.

2.C.525.   Holland, Seamans, comp. **Proceedings of the Fourth Annual
            Conference of the Reading Association of Ireland.**
            Dublin, Ireland: Reading Association of Ireland,
            1979.

2.C.526.   Kellaghan, Thomas.   "Learning Disabilities in Ireland."
            In **Reading Disabilities: An International
            Perspective,** pp. 227-238. Edited by Lester Tarnopol
            and Muriel Tarnopol. Baltimore, Maryland: University
            Park Press, 1976.

2.C.527.   Kellaghan, T., and MacNamara, J. "Reading in a Second
            Language." In **Reading Instruction: An International
            Forum,** pp. 231-240. Edited by M. D. Jenkinson.
            Newark, Delaware: International Reading Association,
            1967.

2.C.528.   Kelly, S. G., and McGee, P. "Survey of Reading
            Comprehension. A Study in Dublin City National
            Schools." **New Res. Ed.** 1:131, 1967.

2.C.529.   Martin, M. O. **Reading Attainment in Irish Primary
            Schools- A Progressive Achievement Gap.** Paper
            presented at The Reading Association of Ireland.
            Dublin: n.p., 1979. ED 178 869.

2.C.530.   McDonagh, D. "A Second Survey of Reading Comprehension
            in Dublin City National Schools." **Irish Journal of
            Education** :   n.d.

2.C.531.   McDonagh, Declan. "A Survey of Reading Comprehension in
            Dublin City Schools." **The Irish Journal of Education**
            7(Summer 1973): 5-10.

2.C.532.   McGee, Patric. "An Examination of Trends in Reading
            Achievement in Dublin Over a Ten-Year Period." In
            Studies in Reading, pp. 27-35. Edited by Vincent
            Greaney. Dublin: The Educational Co., 1977.

2.C.533.   Molloy, Brendan, and Greaney, Vincent. "Reading in the
            Republic of Ireland." **Oideas** 26 (1982): 104-114.

2.C.534.   Molloy, Brendan, and Greaney, Vincent. "Reading in the
            Republic of Ireland: A Bibliography." **Irish Journal
            of Education** 16, (Summer 1982): 3-15.

2.C.535.   Swan, T. Desmond. **Reading Standards in Irish Schools: A
            National Survey of Reading Standards and Related
            Aspects of First Year Pupils in Post-Primary Schools
            in the Republic of Ireland, 1971-72.** Dublin:
            Educational Company of Ireland, 1978.

2.C.536. Travers, Michael. "The Second Replication of a Survey of
          Reading Comprehension in Dublin City Schools." The
          Irish Journal of Education 10, 1+2(Summer/Winter
          1976): 18-22.

2.C.537. Walsh, Sister Marian, comp. Proceedings of the Fifth
          Annual Conference of the Reading Association of
          Ireland. Dublin, Ireland: Reading Association of
          Ireland, 1980.

2.C.538. Ward, Noel. "A Fourth Survey of Reading Comprehension in
          Dublin City National Schools." The Irish Journal of
          Education 16, (Summer 1982): 56-61.

     33. Israel

2.C.539. Adiel, S. "Reading Ability of Culturally Deprived First
          Graders." Megamot (Behavioral Sciences Quarterly)
          15(1968): 345-356 (in Hebrew).

2.C.540. Adoni, Hanna, and Erella Shadmi. "The Portrait of the Citizen
          as a Young Reader: The Function of Books in the
          Political Socialization of Youth in Israel." Reading
          Research Quarterly 16, 1(1980): 121-137.

2.C.541. "The Alphabetic Principle in Hebrew and German Contrasted
          to the Alphabetic Principle in English. See Section
          2.C.23 entry No. 434.

2.C.542. Ben Shach, L. "In the Municipal Library." Second Annual
          Collection of Essays. Jerusalem: Israel Reading
          Association, 1969, pp. 58-61 (in Hebrew).

2.C.543. Bentwich, J. S. Education in Israel. London: Routledge,
          1965.

2.C.544. Braverman, S. "A Phonetic Method for Teaching Reading."
          Urim 25(1968): 115-120 (in Hebrew).

2.C.545. "Changing the Teaching of Reading in Israel." In Ten Years
          of Compensatory Education. Edited by S. Adiel, et al.
          Jerusalem: Ministry of Education, 1970 (in Hebrew).

2.C.546. The Educational System of Israel. Washington, D.C.:
          Institute of International Studies (DHEW/OE), Report
          No.-DHEW-OE-14158. ED 104 742.

2.C.547. Feitelson, Dina. "Causes of Scholastic Failure Among First
          Graders." Megamot Behavioral Sciences Quarterly
          4(1952-1953): 1-84 (in Hebrew).

2.C.548. Feitelson, Dina. "On the Teaching of Reading in Non-
          European Languages." English Language Teaching
          16(1961): 39-43.

2.C.549.   Feitelson, Dina. "Training Teachers of Disadvantaged
             Children." In **Reading, A Human Right and a Human
             Problem**, pp. 141-146. Edited by Ralph C. Staiger and
             Oliver Andresen. Newark, Delaware: International
             Reading Assocation, 1969.

2.C.550.   Feitelson, Diana, and Goldstein, Zahava. "Patterns of
             Book Ownership and Reading to Young Children in
             Israeli School-Oriented and Nonschool-Oriented
             Families." **The Reading Teacher** 39, 9(May 1986): 924-
             930.

2.C.551.   Fijalkow, Jacques. "La Complexite Des Relations Grapho-
             Phonetiques Explique-t-elle Les Difficultes D'
             apprentissage De La Lecture? Le Cas De L'hebreu En
             Israel." **Journal of Research in Reading** 3(February
             1980): 52-59.

2.C.552.   Goldgraber, E. "Reading Instruction in Israel." **Jewish
             Education** 48, (Fall 1980): 16-23.

2.C.553.   Gross, Alice Dzen. "The Relationship Between Sex
             Difference and Reading Ability in an Israeli Kibbutz
             System." In **Cross-Cultural Perspective on Reading and
             Reading Research**, pp. 72-88. Edited by Dina
             Feitelson. Newark, Delaware: International Reading
             Association, 1978.

2.C.554.   Gross, Alice Dzen. "Sex-Role Standards and Reading
             Achievement: A Study of an Israeli Kibbutz System."
             The Reading Teacher 32, 2(November 1978): 149-156.

2.C.555.   Kleinberger, A. F. **Society, Schools and Progress in
             Israel.** Oxford: Pergamon, 1969.

2.C.556.   Kugelmass, Sol, et al. "Perceptual Exploration in Israeli
             Jewish and Bedouin Children." **Journal of Cross-
             Cultural Psychology** 3, 4(December 1972): 345-352.

2.C.557.   Laser-Cohen, Hadara. "A Program for Fostering of Reading
             and Thinking of Disadvantaged Adolescents in Israel."
             Journal of Reading 28, 6(March 1985): 542-549.

2.C.558.   Levy, J., and Blum, U., eds. **Handbook for the First
             Grade.** Tel-Aviv: Urim, 1952 (in Hebrew).

2.C.559.   Lewy, Arieh. "Student Achievement in Israel of Immigrants
             from Developed and Developing Countries." **American
             Educational Research Journal** 18(Spring 1981): 113-
             118.

2.C.560.   Lewy, Arieh, and Davis, D. "What Can Students Read? The
             Level of Reading Mastery in Israeli Schools."
             Comparative Education Review 18, 2(June 1974): 248-
             261.

2.C.561.   Meir, M. "The Use of the School Library." Second Annual
            Collection of Essays. Jerusalem: Israel Reading
            Association, 1969, pp. 51-57 (in Hebrew).

2.C.562.   Venezky, Richard L. The Prereading Skills of Israeli
            Kindergartners. Technical Report No. 332. Madison,
            Wisconsin: Wisconsin University, Research and
            Development Center for Cognitive Learning, 1975.
            ED 113 699.

2.C.563.   Wohl, Aryeh. "No Secrets to Reading: Developing a New
            Reading/Language Arts Learning Program Using
            Television in Israel." The Reading Teacher 38, 4
            (January 1985): 446-449.

        34. Italy

2.C.564.   Lindgren, Scott D., et al. See Section 2.A. entry no. 63.

2.C.565.   Tutolo, Daniel. Beginning Reading in Italy. N.P.: n.p.,
            1980. ED 209 636.

2.C.566.   Zucchermaglio, Cristina, et al. "Literacy and Linguistic
            Awareness: A Study of Italian First Grade Students."
            Reading Psychology 7, 1(1986): 11-25.

        35. Jamaica

2.C.567.   Jennings-Wray, Zelleynne. "Textbook Content and Reading
            Interests of Jamaican Primary School Children."
            Caribbean Journal of Education 9, 3(1982): 188-212.

        36. Japan

2.C.568.   Anzai, E., et al. "Lese-und Schreibstorungen Bei Einem 6
            Jahrigen Knaben." Psychiatria et Neurologia Japonica
            68(1966): 629-640.

2.C.569.   Anzanko, Iwao. "On the Criterion of Book Selection From
            the Viewpoint of Difficulty of Sentence." The Science
            of Reading 1(1956): 29-33.

2.C.570.   Chichii, Katsunori. "Encouraging Broad Reading Among
            Junior High Students in Japan." Journal of Reading
            24, 7(April 1981): 587-590.

2.C.571.   Chu, Yu-Kuang. A Comparative Study of Language Reforms
            in China and Japan. Skidmore College Faculty Research
            Lecture 55-2. Saratoga Springs, New York: Skidmore
            College, 1969.

2.C.572.   Fukuzawa, Shusuke. "Developmental Study on the Factors
           of the Difficulty in Reading Kanji." (Ideographs in
           Japan). The Science of Reading 1(March 1968): 16-
           21.

2.C.573.   Furukawa, James, and Sakamoto, Takahiko. Differences in
           the Rates of Reading Problems in the United States and
           Japan: A Search for Causes. Paper presented at the
           Annual Meeting of the World Congress on Reading.
           Manila: n.p., 1980. ED 199 676.

2.C.574.   Horikawa, Naoyoshi. A Study of Readability in Japanese
           Sentences. Tokyo: Report of the Research Institute
           of the Asahi Shimbun, Asahi Shimbun-sha, 1957.

2.C.575.   Kimura, K. "Zur Erklarung Des Der Japanischen Schrift
           Eigentumlichen Symptombildes." Neurologia 37(1934):
           437-459.

2.C.576.   Kurasawa, Eikichi. "Reading Instruction in Japan." The
           Reading Teacher 16(1962): 13-17.

2.C.577.   Kuromaru, S.; Okada, Y.; et al. "On Developmental Alexia
           and Agraphia." Journal of Pediatrics 25(1962): 853-
           858.

2.C.578.   Mainichi, Shimbun-sha. Report of 1965 Reading Survey.
           Tokyo: Mainichi Shimbunsha, 1966.

2.C.579.   Matsubara, Tatsuya, and Kobayashi, Yoshiro. "A Study on
           Legibility of Kana-Letters." Japanese Journal of
           Psychology 37(1967): 359-363.

2.C.580.   Matsubara, Tatsuya, and Kobayashi, Yoshiro. "Study of
           Legibility of Kana-Letters." Perceptual and Motor
           Skills 25(1967): 36.

2.C.581.   Muraishi, Shozo. "The Reading Ability of Preschool
           Children in Japan." In New Horizons in Reading.
           Proceedings of the Fifth International Reading
           Association World Congress on Reading, pp. 255-268.
           N.P.: n.p., 1976.

2.C.582.   Muraishi, Shozo; Sakamoto, Takahiko; and Kaga, Hideo. "On
           the Criteria for Optimum Type Face." The Science of
           Reading 5(1960): 19-24.

2.C.583.   Muraishi, Shozo; Hideo, Kaga; and Sakamoto, Takahiko. "A
           Study of Legibility of Katakana." Proceedings of the
           Thirtieth Annual Congress of the Japanese Association
           of Applied Psychology, 1963.

2.C.584.   Neville, Mary H. "Learning to Read in Japan." Reading
           12, 1(April 1978): 21-28.

2.C.585.   Obi, I. "Uber Die Angeborene Lese-und Schreibschwache."
            Psychiatria Et Neurologia Japonica 59(1957):   852-867.

2.C.586.   Obonai, Torao, and Sato, Yasumasa. "Two Studies on Read-
            ability." **The Bulletin of the Faculty of Education**
            (Tokyo University of Education) 2(1956):   40-51.

2.C.587.   Okami, Sadao. "A Study of Bibliography on the Delinquent
            (4th Report)- A Case of a Boy Who Left Home." **The
            Science of Reading** 10, 1(1967):   1-7.

2.C.588.   Okami, Sadao. "A Study of Bibliotherapy on the Delinquent
            (5th Report)- A Case of a Sex Offender." **The Science
            of Reading** 10, 2(1967):   9-15.

2.C.589.   Okami, Sadao. "A Study of Bibliotherapy on the Delinquent
            (6th Report)- A Case of Severe Delinquency." **The
            Science of Reading** 10, 3(1967):   18-24.

2.C.590.   Okami, Sadao. "A Study of Bibliotherapy on the Delinquent
            (9th Report)." **The Science of Reading** 11, 3(1968):
            22-28.

2.C.591.   Okami, Sadao. "A Study of Bibliotherapy (8th Report)- A
            Case of Enuresis Nocturna." **The Science of Reading**
            11, 1-2(1968):   48-51.

2.C.592.   Pieronek, Florence T. "Teaching Reading in Japanese
            Elementary Schools." **The Reading Teacher** 31, 5
            (February 1978):   511-513.

2.C.593.   Rai, Akiko. "An Experimental Study on the Change of
            Opinion Caused by Reading." **The Science of Reading**
            10, 1(1967):   26-35.

2.C.594.   Sakamoto, Ichiro. **The Sakamoto Reading Readiness Test.**
            Tokyo: Maki Shoten, 1953 (in English).

2.C.595.   Sakamoto, Ichiro. **Basic Vocabularies for Education.**
            Tokyo: Maki Shoten, 1958.

2.C.596.   Sakamoto, Ichiro. "Assessing the Vocabulary Weight of
            Sentences--An Attempt to Approach Readability." **The
            Science of Reading** 6, 1-2)1962):   37-44.

2.C.597.   Sakamoto, Ichiro. "Assessing the Weight of Sentence
            Length--An Attempt to Approach Readability." **The
            Science of Reading** 8, 1(1964):   1-6.

2.C.598.   Sakamoto, Ichiro. "The Scope of Reading in Japan." In
            Reading Instruction: An International Forum, pp. 33-
            43. Edited by M. D. Jenkinson. Newark, Delaware:
            International Reading Association, 1967.

2.C.599.   Sakamoto, Ichiro; Fujii, Masumi; Tsutsumi, Yoshiko; and
            Arai, Yoshiko. "Picture Books with Infants." **The**

Science of Reading 12, 2(1969):   23-29.

2.C.600.   Sakamoto, Ichiro; Hayashi, Kumiko; and Kamei, Michiko. "A
            Developmental Study on the Points of Inspiration in
            Reading." The Science of Reading 10, 3(1967): 1-9.

2.C.601.   Sakamoto, Ichrio; Ishii, Masako; and Kuratani, Michiko.
            "An Attempt to Diagnose Children's Attitudes in
            Reading Stories." The Science of Reading 12, 3(1969):
            17-27.

2.C.602.   Sakamoto, Ichiro; Matsumoto, Ritsuko; Nakamure, Yoshiko;
            and Shimada, Sanae. "Case Studies on Bibliotherapy
            Applied to Emotionally Unstable Pupils." The Science
            of Reading 11, 1-2(1968): 52-65.

2.C.603.   Sakamoto, S. "A Contribution to Kanji- Kana Problem in
            Dyslexia." Bulletin of Asaka Medical Association 4
            (1940): 185-212.

2.C.604.   Sakamoto, Takahiko. "The Affect of Kanji on the Read-
            ability of the Japanese Sentences." Master's Thesis,
            Tokyo University of Education, 1960.

2.C.605.   Sakamoto, Takahiko. "On Reading Skills of Vertical Versus
            Horizontal Sentences." Unpublished paper read at The
            Third Annual Congress of the Japanese Association of
            Educational Psychology. Nagoya, Japan: n.p., 1961.

2.C.606.   Sakamoto, Takahiko. "Space Between Letters and Lines,
            Words Per Line in Lateral Writing." Scientific Asahi
            25, 2(1965): 91-95.

2.C.607.   Sakamoto, Takahiko. "Legibility of Print in Lateral
            Writing." Scientific Asahi 26, 3(1966): 39-46.

2.C.608.   Sakamoto, Takahiko. "Problem Children in Reading." The
            Bulletin of the Nama Institute of Educational Research
            26(1969): 1-22.

2.C.609.   Sakamoto, Takahiko. "Preschool Reading in Japan." The
            Reading Teacher 29, 3(December 1975): 240-244.

2.C.610.   Sakamoto, Takahiko, and Makita, Kiyoshi. "Japan." In
            Comparative Reading, pp. 440-465. Edited by John
            Downing. New York: Macmillan, 1973.

2.C.611.   Sakamoto, Takahiko; Muraishi, Shozo; and Kaga, Hideo. "A
            Study of Legibility of Kana." Proceedings of the 28th
            Annual Congress of the Japanese Association of Applied
            Psychology, 1961.

2.C.612.   Sakamoto, Takahiko; Shozo, Muraishi; and Kaga, Hideo. "A
            Study of Legibility of Katakana." Proceedings of the
            28th Annual Congress of the Japanese Association of
            Applied Psychology, 1961.

2.C.613.   Sakamoto, Takahiko, and Takagi, Kazuko. "A Study of
            Disabled Readers." **The Science of Reading** 11, 1-2
            (1968): 1-15.

2.C.614.   Sheridan, E. Marcia. "Early Reading in Japan." **Reading
            World** 21, 4(May 1982): 326-332.

2.C.615.   Shuppan, Kagaku Kenkyu-sho. **Children and Reading.** Tokyo:
            Shuppan Kagaku Kenkyu-sho, 1968.

2.C.616.   Steinberg, Danny D., and Yamada, Jun. "Pigs Will be
            Chickens: Reply to Tzeng and Singer." **Reading
            Research Quarterly** 14, 4(1978-1979): 668-671.

2.C.617.   Stevenson, Harold W., et al. See Section 2.A. entry no.
            92.

2.C.618.   Takagi, Kazuko. "Interest in Picture Books of Japanese
            Five Year Olds." **The Reading Teacher** 33, 4(January
            1980): 442-444.

2.C.619.   Taylor, W. L. "Cloze Procedure: A New Tool for Measuring
            Readability." **Journalism Quarterly** 30(1953): 415-
            433.

2.C.620.   Toyama, Shigehiko. "New Tendency in Japanese Reading: An
            Oral Style." **Journal of Reading** 21, 3(December 1977):
            253-254.

2.C.621.   Tzeng, Ovid J. L., and Singer, Harry. "Failure of
            Steinberg and Yamada to Demostrate Superiority of
            Kanji Over Kana for Initial Reading Instruction in
            Japan." **Reading Research Quarterly** 14, 4(1978-1979):
            661-667.

2.C.622.   UNESCO. See Section 2.A. entry no. 103.

       37. Kenya

2.C.623.   Wanoike, E. N. **A Teacher Training Methodology Manual
            in Kiswahili for Lower Primary Classes in Kenya.** N.P.,
            1982.

       38. Kuwait

2.C.624.   Kharma, N.N. "Attempt to Individualize the Reading Skill
            at Kuwait University." **English Language Teaching
            Journal** 35, (July 1981): 398-404.

       39. Lebanon

2.C.625.   Adams, Effie Kaye. "Reading Interests of UNRWA Students
            in Lebanon." 18th Yearbook, **National Reading Con-**

ference: The Psychology of Reading Behavior.
Milwaukee: The National Reading Conference, 1969.

40. Madagascar

2.C.626.   Stolee, P. B. "Learning to Read in Madagascar." **Reading
            Improvement** 7, (Winter 1970): 84-86.

41. Malaysia

2.C.627.   Mustapha, Nik Faizah. "Case Study: Malaysia." In **A
            Reason to Read: A Report on an International
            Symposium on the Promotion of the Reading Habit,** pp.
            47-49. New York: Academy for Educational Development
            and UNESCO, 1976.

42. Mexico

2.C.628.   Herbert, C. H. Jr. "Bilingual Child's Right to Read."
            Claremont Reading Conference Yearbook, 36, 1972, 50-
            58.

2.C.629.   Hinds, Harold E., Jr. "Review Essay: If You've Been to
            Mexico Lately, Did You Notice What Most Mexicans Are
            Reading? Would You Believe It's Comics and Photo-
            Novels?" **Canadian and International Education** 11,
            (1982): 73-79.

2.C.630.   Miller, Robert. "Public Primary School Education in Mexico:
            A Focus on Reading Instruction in Mexico City."
            Dissertation Abstracts V41(04), Sec. A., P1510, 1980.

2.C.631.   Miller, R. "Mexican Approach to Developing Bilingual
            Materials and Teaching Literacy to Bilingual
            Students." **The Reading Teacher** 35, (April 1982): 800-
            804.

2.C.632.   Miller, Robert. "Reading Instruction and Primary School
            Education: Mexican Teachers' Viewpoints." **The
            Reading Teacher** 35, 8(May 1982): 890-894.

2.C.633.   Shachter, Jacqueline N. "The Effect of Studying Literary
            Translations on Sixth-grade Pupils' Knowledge of
            Mexican Culture." **Social Education** 36, 2(February
            1972): 162-167.

43. Nepal

2.C.634.   Chacko, Chinna. "Production of Reading Materials: A
            Comparative Study." In **Reading: A Human Right and a
            Human Problem,** pp. 87-92. Edited by Ralph C. Staiger
            and Oliver Andresen. Newark, Delaware: International

Reading Association, 1969.

2.C.635.   Junge, Barbara, and Shrestha, Shashi M. "Another Barrier
            Broken: Teaching Village Girls to Read in Nepal."
            The Reading Teacher 37, 9(May 1984): 846-852.

2.C.636.   Matthias, Margaret, and Quisenberry, James D. "Toward
            Increasing Literacy in Developing Countries." Child-
            hood Education 62, 3(January/February 1986): 196-190.

        44. Netherlands

2.C.637.   Dumont, Joep J. "Learning Disabilities in the
            Netherlands." In Reading Disabilities: An Inter-
            national Perspective, pp. 239-248. Edited by Lester
            Tarnopol and Muriel Tarnopol. Baltimore, Maryland:
            University Park Press, 1976.

2.C.638.   Kramer, K. "Word Study Skills in Iowa and the
            Netherlands.." Elementary School Journal 61(November
            1960): 81-85.

        45. New Zealand

2.C.639.   Barney, W. D. "Flexibility in Introductions to Reading:
            Some Reflections on New Zealand Practices."
            Conference on Reading, University of Pittsburgh
            Reports 19(1963): 39-46.

2.C.640.   Clay, Marie M. "Emergent Reading Behavior." Doctoral
            Disseration, University of Aukland, 1966. (Summarized
            in "The Reading Behavior of Five Year Old Children."
            New Zealand Journal of Educational Studies 2, 1(1967):
            11-31. Edited by Marie Clay.)

2.C.641.   Clay, Marie. "Language Skills: A Comparison of Maori,
            Samoan, and Pakeha Children Aged 5 to 7 Years." New
            Zealand Journal of Educational Studies 5(1970): 153-
            162.

2.C.642.   Clay, Marie M. "Early Childhood and Cultural Diversity in
            New Zealand." The Reading Teacher 29, 4(January
            1976): 332-342.

2.C.643.   Clay, Marie M., ed. "The Reading Behavior of Five Year
            Old Children." New Zealand Journal of Educational
            Studies 2, 1(1967): 11-31.

2.C.644.   Foster, Marion E., et al. See Section 2.C.9 entry no.
            206.

2.C.645.   Galloway, David, and Barrett, Colleen. "Factors Associated
            with Suspension from New Zealand Secondary Schools."
            Educational Review 36, 3(November 1984): 277-285.

2.C.646.   Guthrie, John. "Reading in New Zealand." Reading
           Research Quarterly 17, 1(1981): 6-27.

2.C.647.   Holdaway, D. "Shared Book Experience: Teaching Reading
           Using Favorite Books." Theory into Practice 21,
           (Autumn 1982): 293-300.

2.C.648.   McCreary, J. R. "Reading Tests with Maori Children." New
           Zealand Journal of Educational Studies 1(1966): 40-50.

2.C.649.   Trevor, Ruth. "An Eclectic Approach to Beginning
           Reading." In Reading: A Human Right and a Human
           Problem, pp. 34-38. Edited by Ralph C. Staiger and
           Oliver Andresen. Newark, Delaware: International
           Reading Association, 1969.

   46. Nigeria

2.C.650.   Abiri, J. O. O. "World Initial Teaching Alphabet Versus
           Traditional Orthography." Doctoral dissertation,
           University of Ibadan, Nigeria, 1969.

2.C.651.   Abiri, J. O. O. "Using W.I.T.A. and Standard Orthography
           in Teaching English Reading in Nigeria." The Reading
           Teacher 30, (November 1976): 137-140.

2.C.652.   Abiri, J. O. O. "Reading in Nigeria." The Reading Teacher
           30, (February 1977): 509-514.

2.C.653.   Adeniran, A., and Unoh, S. O. "Comparative Study of Read-
           ing Achievement in English and Yoruba." West African
           Journal of Education 19(October 1975): 391-401.

2.C.654.   Balogun, I. O. B. "The Intellectual and Residential
           Correlates of Reading Achievement in Nigerian
           Secondary Schools." West African Journal of Education
           20(June 1976): 245-256.

2.C.655.   Gbenedio, U. V. "Two Methods of Teaching Reading in
           Nigerian Primary Classes." ELT Journal 40, 1(January
           1986): 46-51.

2.C.656.   McKillop, Anne, and Yoloye, E. A. "The Reading of
           University Students." Teacher Education 3(November
           1962): 93-107.

2.C.657.   Obah, T. Y. "Reading in Higher Education in Nigeria:
           Problems and Progress." Journal of Reading 25,
           (January 1982): 315-321.

2.C.658.   Odebunmi, Akin. "Adult Education and Literacy in
           Nigeria." In Yearbook of the 45th Claremont College
           Reading Conference. Edited by Malcolm P. Douglass.
           Claremont, California: Claremont Reading Conference,
           1981.

2.C.659.   Odejide, Biola, and James, Sybil L. "Nigerian Children's
            Books for Intercultural Understanding in the English
            Speaking World." Journal of Reading 25, 6(March
            1982): 517-524.

2.C.660.   Tabachnick, B. Robert. Reading English in Nigerian
            Primary Schools: Gateway to Understanding. 32nd
            Claremont Reading Conference. Edited by Malcolm P.
            Douglass. Claremont, California: Claremont College
            Reading Conference, 1968.

2.C.661.   Taiwo, Oladele. "The Problem of Beginning and Develop-
            mental Reading in Nigeria Primary Schools." In Mother
            Tongue or Second Language? Edited by Dina Feitelson.
            Newark, Delaware: International Reading Association,
            1979.

2.C.662.   Williams, D. "Factors Related to Performance in Reading
            English as a Second Language." Language Learning 31,
            (June 1981): 31-50.

        47. Northern Ireland

2.C.663.   Gray, Betty. "A Survey of Books Used in Northern Ireland
            to Teach Beginners to Read." Northern Teacher 14,
            1(Autumn 1983): 28-32.

2.C.664.   Wilson, John A. Reading Standards in Northern Ireland.
            Belfast: Northern Ireland Council for Educational
            Research, 1973.

2.C.665.   Wilson, John A. Reading Standards in 1976. Belfast: The
            Northern Ireland Council for Educational Research,
            1977.

        48. Norway

2.C.666.   Gjessing, Hans-Jorgen. "The Concept of Reading Readiness
            in Norway." In Reading Instruction: An International
            Forum, pp. 70-79. Edited by Marion D. Jenkinson.
            Newark, Delaware: International Reading Association,
            1967.

2.C.667.   Hagtvedt, G. A. "A Comparison of Approaches to Reading
            Disability in the Elementary Grades in Norway and
            Ohio." Master's thesis, The Ohio State University,
            1972.

2.C.668.   Matejcek, Z., and Vokounova, A. "Letter Confusion in
            Norwegian and Czech Children." Australian Journal of
            Remedial Education 14, 1(1982): 47-51.

2.C.669.   Peters, F. J. J. "Norwegian TV--A Continuing Reading
            Program." Journal of Reading 18, 3(December 1974):

200-202.

2.C.670.   Preus, Alf. "Working with Reading Problems in Norway."
            Reading Horizons 3(1962-1963): 1-20.

2.C.671.   Skjelfjord, V. J. "Teaching Children to Segment Spoken
            Words as an Aid in Learning to Read." Journal of
            Learning Disabilities 9, (May 1976): 297-306.

2.C.672.   Vik, Grete Hagtvedt. "Reading Disabilities in Norwegian
            Elementary Grades." In Reading Disabilities: An
            International Perspective, pp. 249-264. Edited by
            Lester Tarnopol and Muriel Tarnopol. Baltimore,
            Maryland: University Park Press, 1976.

    49. Oman

2.C.673.   Al-Barwani, Thuwayba Ahmad. A Process for Developing
            Policy Recommendations for the Recruitment and
            Retention of Learners in Literacy Education Programs:
            The Oman Experience. Ann Arbor, Michigan: Disserta-
            tion Abstracts, 42(12), Sec. A. P4999, 1981.

    50. Papua New Guinea

2.C.674.   Downing, John. "A Source of Cognitive Confusion for
            Beginning Readers: Learning in a Second Language."
            The Reading Teacher 37, (January 1984): 366-370.

2.C.675.   Downing, John, and Downing, Marianne. Experiments in
            Linguistics and Literacy in Papua New Guinea.
            Victoria, British Columbia: University of Victoria
            Faculty of Education, 1986.

2.C.676.   McCallum, C. R. "Reading Competence of Pupils in Primary
            Schools in Papua, New Guinea." New Guinea Psychologist
            5, 3(December 1973): 110-116.

2.C.677.   Moore, Dennis W., and O'Driscoll, Michael P. "Strategies
            for Studying Text: A Comparison of Papua New Guinea
            and American Research Findings." Journal of
            Educational Psychology 75, 3(June 1983): 460-464.

2.C.678.   Price, J. Jr. "Studies of Reading in Papua New Guinea."
            Papua New Guinea Journal of Education 19, 1(March
            1974): 21-27.

2.C.679.   Smithies, Michael. "Reading Habits at a Third World
            Technological University." Reading in a Foreign
            Language 1, 2(October 1983): 111-118.

51. Peru

2.C.680.   Caceres, N. R. "Teaching of Reading Peru." The Reading
            Teacher 16, (September 1962): 18-21.

2.C.681.   Nemeth, Edward J. The Educational System of Peru.
            Washington, D.C.: Office of Education (DHEW), Report
            No.-OE-77-19129. 1977. ED 148 685.

2.C.682.   Yabar-Dextre, P. "Choosing a Language of Instruction in
            Peru." International Review of Education 24, 3(1978):
            406-409.

52. Philippines

2.C.683.   Gonzales, Andrew, and Rafael, Teresita C. "Transitional
            Reading Problems in English in a Philippine Bilingual
            Setting." The Reading Teacher 35, 3(December 1981):
            281-286.

2.C.684.   Gonzales, Esperanza A. "A Reading Program for the Gifted
            in the Philippines." Journal of Reading 24, 8(May
            1981): 707-711.

2.C.685.   Maminta, Rosario E. "A Comparative Structural Analysis of
            The Oral Language Materials and the Basic Readers Used
            in Philippine Schools." International Reading
            Association Conference Proceedings, Part 1, 13(April
            1968): 878-884.

2.C.686.   Morales, A. T., et al. Achievement and Self-Discovery.
            Boston: Ginn, 1954.

2.C.687.   Solis, M. M., et al. Teaching the Filipino Child to Read.
            Manila: Bureau of Public Schools, 1955.

2.C.688.   Tensuan, E. S., and Davis, F. B. "Experiment with Two
            Methods of Teaching Reading." The Reading Teacher 18,
            (October 1964): 8-15.

2.C.689.   Tensuan, E. S., and Davis, F. B. "Psychology of Beginning
            Reading: An Experiment with Two Methods." British
            Journal of Educational Psychology 35, (June 1965):
            127-139.

53. Rhodesia (See Zimbabwe)

54. Samoa

2.C.690.   Cope, I. L. "Teaching Reading in Samoa." National Edu-
            cation Association Journal 50, (January 1961): 51.

55. Scotland

2.C.691.   Andersen, Irving H. et al. See Section 2.C.17. entry no.
            273.

2.C.692.   Blythman, M. "Reading and Language Comprehension: What
            Is going on in Scotland's Primary Schools?" Viewpoints
            in Teaching and Learning 54, (July 1978): 117-126.

2.C.693.   Booth, Gordon K. "Effects of Length of Schooling Upon
            Early Reading Attainment." Educational Research 23,
            1(November 1980): 57-58.

2.C.694.   Clark, Margaret M. Reading Difficulties in Schools.
            London: Heinemann Educational Books, 1979. ED 177
            504.

2.C.695.   Elder, Richard D. See Section 2.A. entry no. 19.

2.C.696.   Gatherer, W. A. "Reading and Language Comprehension: What
            is Going on In Scottish Secondary Schools?" Viewpoints
            in Teaching and Learning 54, (July 1978): 127-138.

2.C.697.   Goodacre, Elizabeth J. et al. See Section 2.C.17. entry
            no. 324.

2.C.698.   Maxwell, James. Reading Progress from 8 to 15: A Survey
            of Attainment and Teaching Practices in Scotland.
            Windsor: NFER; Atlantic Highlands, New Jersey: Dis-
            tributed by Humanities Press, 1977.

2.C.699.   Nisbet, John; Welsh, Jennifer; and Watt, Joyce. "Reading
            Standards in Aberdeen 1962-1972." Educational
            Research 16(June 1974): 172-175.

2.C.700.   Personke, C. "Spelling Achievement of Scottish and
            American Children." Elementary School Journal 66
            (March 1966): 337-343.

2.C.701.   Pont, H. B. "Investigation into the Use of the S.R.A.
            Reading Laboratory in Three Midlothian Schools."
            Educational Research 8, (June 1966): 230-236.

2.C.702.   Russell, D. R. See Section 2.C.17 entry no. 374.

2.C.703.   Scottish Council for Research in Education. See Section
            2.C.17 entry no. 378.

2.C.704.   Scottish Education Department. Primary Education in
            Scotland. Edinburgh: H.M.S.O., 1965.

56. Senegal

2.C.705.   Burley, JoAnne E., et al. "A Report on the Reading Habits
            of College-Aged Senegalese Students." Paper presented
            at the Annual Meeting of the International Reading

Association. Atlanta: 1984. ED 246 411.

57. Sierra Leone

2.C.706.   Brams, Patricia. "Reading Between the Lines: Societal
             Norms in Sierra Leonian Readers." **International
             Review of Education** 26, 4(1980): 483–500.

58. Singapore

2.C.707.   Moi, Ng Seok. "Reading Acquisition in Singapore."
             Singapore Journal of Education 6, 2(1984): 15–20.

2.C.708.   Moore, Betty Jean. "English Reading Skills of Multilingual
             Pupils in Singapore." **The Reading Teacher** 35, 6(March
             1982): 696–701.

2.C.709.   National Book Development Council of Singapore. **First
             National Readership Survey.** National Book Development
             Council of Singapore, 1981.

2.C.710.   Ng, S. M., and Khoo, M. "Researching Early Reading
             Progress in Singapore." In **Research and Educational
             Futures: Technology Development and Educational
             Futures.** Papers of the National Conference. Perth:
             Australian Association for Research in Education, 1984.

59. South Africa

2.C.711.   Butterfield, Paul H. "Read, Educate and Develop—the READ
             Project in South Africa." **International Review of
             Education** 30, 4(1984): 479–484.

2.C.712.   Logue, George D. "Learning Disabilities in the Republic
             of South Africa." In **Reading Disabilities: An Inter-
             national Perspective**, pp. 269–285. Edited by Lester
             Tarnopol and Muriel Tarnopol. Baltimore, Maryland:
             University Park Press, 1976.

2.C.713.   Neville, Mary H. "Reading in Capetown Schools: A
             Comparative View." **Comparative Education** 10, 2(June
             1974): 115–120.

2.C.714.   Pienaar, P. T. "Using the Language Experience Approach in
             Special Classes in South Africa." **The Reading Teacher**
             31, (October 1977): 60–66.

60. South Korea

2.C.715.   Hong, Woong Sun. **Review and Perspective of Reading
             Education in Korea.** Paper presented at the Seoul
             International Seminar on Reading, August 1976.

2.C.716.   Kim, Byongwon. "Reading and Reading Instruction in Korea:
            Past and Present." In **Mother Tongue or Second
            Language.** Edited by Dina Feitelson. Newark,
            Delaware: International Reading Association, 1979.

2.C.717.   **National Assessment of Students Achievement Progress.
            Elementary and Middle School.** Korea: Korean
            Educational Development Institute, 1975 (in Korean).

     61. South Vietnam

2.C.718.   Nguyen Quy Bong. "Beginning Reading in South Vietnam."
            In **The 35th Yearbook of the Claremont College Reading
            Conference.** Edited by Malcolm P. Douglass. Claremont
            College Reading Conference, 1971.

     62. Soviet Union

2.C.719.   Belikova, A. V. "Siberian Textbooks in the 1920s and Their
            Role in Developing the Sociopolitical and Labor
            Activism of Pupils." **Soviet Education** 24, 1(November
            1981): 29-37.

2.C.720.   Curriculum-Methods Administration. "The Literature
            Curriculum for the Fifth Grade (68 Class Hours)."
            Soviet Education 18, 9-11(July-September 1976): 68-
            72.

2.C.721.   Curriculum-Methods Administration. "The Literature
            Curriculum for the Sixth Grade (68 Hours)." **Soviet
            Education** 18, 9-11(July-September 1976): 94-100.

2.C.722.   Department of Methods for Teaching Literature.
            "Concerning Literature Textbooks. (Grades 4-7)."
            Soviet Education 18, 9-11(July-September 1976): 120-
            130.

2.C.723.   Downing, J. "Reading Research and Instruction in the
            U.S.S.R." **The Reading Teacher** 37, (March 1984): 598-
            603.

2.C.724.   Durr, W. K., and Hickman, R. "Reading Instruction in
            Soviet Schools." **The Reading Teacher** 28, (November
            1974): 134-140.

2.C.725.   Elkonin, D. B. "USSR." In **Comparative Reading,** pp. 551-
            579. Edited by John Downing. New York: Macmillan,
            1973.

2.C.726.   Galperin, P. J. "An Investigation of the Development of
            Mental Operations." **Psychological Science in the**
            USSR 1(1959).

2.C.727.   Gromtseva, S. N. "Model Planning of Literature Lessons in
            the Tenth Grade for the 1973/74 School Year." Soviet
            Education 18, 9-11(July-September 1976):   195-252.

2.C.728.   Hildreth, Gertrude. "Reading with a Rational Alphabet:
            the Russian System." The Reading Teacher 22(December
            1968):   251-261.

2.C.729.   Hopkins, Elaine. "Literature in the Schools of the Soviet
            Union." Comparative Education 10, 1(March 1974):
            25-34.

2.C.730.   Kachurin, M. G., and Shneerson, M. A. "Recommended
            Methods for Planning Literature Lessons in the Eighth
            Grade (1974/75 School Year)." Soviet Education 18,
            9-11(July-September 1976):   131-194.

2.C.731.   Kachurin, M. G., and Shneerson, M. A. "Recommended Methods
            for Planning Literature Lessons in the Ninth Grade
            (1974/75 School Year)." Soviet Education 18, 9-11
            (July-September 1976):   195-252.

2.C.732.   Khokhlova, N. A. The Comparative Psychological Study of
            the Sound Analysis of Pre-School Children. Diploma
            dissertation, Faculty of Psychology, Lomonosov, The
            Moscow State University, 1955.

2.C.733.   Kudriashev, N. I. "Certain Trends in the Development of
            Literary Education in Secondary School." Soviet
            Education 18, 9-11(July-September 1976):   6-20.

2.C.734.   Kurdivmova, T. F. "On the Ways and Means of Studying
            Literature in the Fourth Grade." Soviet Education 18,
            9-11(July-September 1976):   53-67.

2.C.735.   Loshkareva, Nelli Anisimova. "Improving Reading Techniques
            in the U.S.S.R. Prospects 15, 1(1985):   111-118.

2.C.736.   Luria, A. R. Traumatic Aphasia. Moscow: Academy of
            Medical Science of the USSR, 1947.

2.C.737.   Morton, M. "Mass Culture and Elite Readers in Soviet
            Society." Claremont Reading Conference Yearbook, 36,
            1972, 32-43.

2.C.738.   Olshannikova, A. E. "The Development of the Generalized
            Mental Operation of Sound Discrimination." Reports of
            the Academy of Psychological Science of the Russian
            Soviet Federative Socialist Republic 3(1958).

2.C.739.   Shvatchkin, N. Kh. "The Development of Phonematic
            Perception of Speech in Young Children." News of the
            Academy of Psychological Science of the Russian Soviet
            Federative Socialist Republic 13(1948).

2.C.740.   Snezhevskaia, M. A. "The Sixth-Grade Literature Course."
            Soviet Education 18, 9-11(July-September 1976): 101-
            119.

2.C.741.   Thall, M. "Teaching Reading in the Soviet Union." The
            Reading Teacher 25, (March 1972): 523-527.

2.C.742.   Trace, A. S., Jr. "Reading Program in Soviet Schools."
            Phi Delta Kappan 43, (March 1962): 259-262.

2.C.743.   Ungaro, D. "Can Ivan Help Johnny Read? Russian Reading
            Program." Elementary English 51, (September 1974):
            846-852.

2.C.744.   Zepalova, T. S. "On the Fifth Grade Literature Course."
            Soviet Education 18, 9-11(July-September 1976): 73-
            93.

2.C.745.   Zhinkin, N. I. The Mechanism of Speech. Moscow: Academy
            of Psychological Science of the Russian Soviet Feder-
            ative Socialist Republic, 1958.

2.C.746.   Zhurova, L. E., and Elkonin, D. B. "On the Question of
            the Phonematic Perception of Children of Preschool
            Age." In The Symposium, Education at the Preschool
            Age Level. Moscow: Academy of Psychological Science
            of the Russian Soviet Federative Socialist Republic,
            1963.

63. Sweden

2.C.747.   Hansson, G. "Further Implications of the I.E.A. Studies in
            the Mother Tongue: The Swedish Case." Research in
            the Teaching of English 10, (Spring 1976): 22-30.

2.C.748.   Grundin, Hans U. Las-och Skrivformagans Utveckling Genom
            Skolaren (The Development of Reading and Writing
            Skills Through the School Years), SO Report No. 20.
            Stockholm: Liber Laromedel, 1977.

2.C.749.   Malmquist, Eve. Factors Related to Reading Disabilities
            in the First Grade of the Elementary School.
            Stockholm: 1960.

2.C.750.   Malmquist, Eve. Barnens Kunskaper Och Fardigheter Vid
            Skolgangens Borjan (Research Report No. 1 From the
            National School for Educational Research). Stockholm:
            Kungl. Skoloverstyrelsen, 1961.

2.C.751.   Malmquist, E. "Teaching of Reading the First Grade in
            Swedish Schools." The Reading Teacher 16, (September
            1962): 22-28.

2.C.752.   Malmquist, E. "Recent Developments in Reading in Sweden."
            Chicago: Conference on Reading 27, (1965): 102-111.

2.C.753.   Malmquist, Eve. Jag Kan Lasa. Stockholm: Natur Och
            Kultur, 1967-1969 (Books 1-5).

2.C.754.   Malmquist, E. "Diagnostic and Predictive Measures in the
            Teaching of Reading in Sweden." International Reading
            Association Conference Papers 14, 1970, 249-259.

2.C.755.   Malmquist, Eve. Las-och Skrivsvarigheter Hos Barn.
            Analys Och Behandlingsmetodik. Lund: Gleerups
            Bokforlag, 1971.

2.C.756.   Malmquist, Eve. "Sweden." In Comparative Reading, pp.
            466-487. Edited by John Downing. New York:
            Macmillan, 1973.

2.C.757.   Malmquist, Eve. Beginning Reading in Sweden. Paper
            presented at the Annual Meeting of the International
            Reading Association World Congress on Reading.
            Hamburg: n.p., 1978. ED 169 470.

2.C.758.   Malmquist, Eve. "Reading Research and the Teaching of
            Reading in Sweden." In Cross-Cultural Perspectives
            on Reading and Reading Research, pp. 133-143. Edited
            by Dina Feitelson. Newark, Delaware: International
            Reading Association, 1978.

2.C.759.   Malmquist, Eve. "An Example of a Cross-National Study on
            Primary Reading." In Handbook on Comparative Reading.
            Compiled by Eve Malmquist. Newark, Delaware: Inter-
            national Reading Association, 1982.

2.C.760.   Marklund, Sixten. "Comparative School Research and the
            Swedish School Reform." International Review of
            Education 17, 1(1971): 39-48.

2.C.761.   Weibull, Lennart. Periodicals in Politics: Results from
            a Swedish Survey.. Gothenburg, Sweden: Gothenburg
            University Institute of Political Science, 1977. ED
            144 058.

64. Switzerland

2.C.762.   Neville, M. R. "Beginning Reading in a Second Language
            in Switzerland." The Reading Teacher 22, (May 1969):
            739-741.

65. Taiwan

2.C.763.   Smith, Nancy J. "Remedial Instruction in Taiwan: A Model
            for Using the Reader Effectively." The Reading Teacher
            36, 1(October 1982): 34-27.

2.C.764.   Stevenson, Harold W., et al. See Section 2.A. entry no. 92.

66. Thailand

2.C.765.   Amatyakul, Kiatiwan. Participation in Adult Education: A
            Case and Pilot Study of a Functional Literacy and
            Family Life Planning Program in Thailand. Ann Arbor,
            Michigan: Dissertation Abstracts, 41(03), Sec. A,
            P0893, 1980.

2.C.766.   Nilagupta, Sirirat. "The Relationship of Syntax to Read-
            ability for ESL Students in Thailand." In Cross-
            Cultural Perspectives on Reading and Reading Research,
            pp. 89-102. Edited by Dina Feitelson. Newark,
            Delaware: International Reading Association, 1978.

2.C.767.   Pongnoi, Nakorn. "Reading Centers in Remote Areas." In
            Reading: A Human Right and a Human Problem, pp. 112-
            118. Edited by Ralph C. Staiger and Oliver Andresen.
            Newark, Delaware: International Reading Association,
            1969.

2.C.768.   Pongnoi, N. "Reading Changes Lives: The Hills of
            Thailand." Journal of Reading 19, (March 1976): 475-
            480.

2.C.769.   Sungkchad, Kochgorn. "Performance Requirements for Adult
            Functional Literacy Teachers in Thailand as Perceived
            by Adult Functional Literacy Teachers and the
            Volunteer Teachers from the Flatlands and the Hill-
            tribes and Supervisors in Adult Education."
            Dissertation Abstracts, V42(09), Sec. A., P3840, 1981.

67. Turkey

2.C.770.   Hildreth, G. "How Turkish Children Learn to Read."
            Elementary School Journal 61, (October 1960): 14-23.

68. Tunisia

2.C.771.   The Educational System of Tunisia. Washington, D.C.:
            Office of Education (DHEW), Report No.-DHEW-OE-74-
            19109. ED 104 737.

69. United States

2.C.772.   Aaron, Ira E. "What Teachers and Prospective Teachers
            Know About Phonics Generalizations." Journal of
            Educational Research 53(May 1960): 323-330.

2.C.773.   Acland, Henry. "A Policy Analysis of Reading Achievement
            in ECE Schools and non-ECE Schools." Studies in
            Educational Evaluation 3(Winter 1977): 195-206.

2.C.774.   Adams, Effie Kay. See Section 2.C.39. entry no. 625.

2.C.775.   Allen, James E., Jr. "Target for the 70's." American
            Education 5(December 1969): 2-4.

2.C.776.   Amatyakul, Kiatiwan. See Section 2.C.66 entry no. 765.

2.C.777.   Anderson, Irving H. et al. See Section 2.C.17 entry no.
            273.

2.C.778.   Archer, Julie, et al. See Section 2.C.23 entry no. 435.

2.C.779.   Arizona, Department of Education. Third Grade Reading
            Achievement Test Result Report. Phoenix: Arizona
            Department of Education, n.d.

2.C.780.   Austin, Mary C. "United States." In Comparative Reading,
            pp. 488-550. Edited by John Downing. New York:
            Macmillan, 1973.

2.C.781.   Austin, Mary C., and Smith Carl B. Survey of Title I
            Reading Programs in the Fiscal Year of 1966. Cleveland:
            Case Western Research University, U.S. Office of
            Education Contract 3-7-000168, Final Report, 1967.

2.C.782.   Balch, Rita B; Knych, Betty J.; and McGinnis, Mary L.
            "Remedial Instruction in the Virgin Island of the
            United States." In Reading Disabilities: An Inter-
            national Perspective, pp. 327-334. Edited by Lester
            Tarnopol and Muriel Tarnopol. Baltimore, Maryland:
            University Park Press, 1976.

2.C.783.   Bean, Thomas W. "Oral Reading Miscues of Hawaiian Islands
            Dialect Speakers in Grades Four, Five, and Six."
            Reading Improvement 15, 2(Summer 1978): 115-118.

2.C.784.   Berger, A. See Section 2.C.9. entry no. 205.

2.C.785.   Bordeaux, Elizabeth A., and Shope, Nathaniel H. An Eval-
            uation of Three Approaches to Teaching Reading in
            First Grade. Goldsboro, North Carolina: Goldsboro
            City Schools and the North Carolina Department of
            Public Instruction, Raleigh. 19?.

2.C.786.   Boykin, A Wade. "Reading Achievement and the Social-
            Cultural Frame of Reference of Afro-American Children."
            Journal of Negro Education 53, 4(Fall 1984): 464-473.

2.C.787.   Bremer, Neville Hasso. A Comparative Study of Children's
            Achievements in Reading in Grade One Under Certain
            Selected Conditions in the Amarillo, Texas Public
            Schools. Ann Arbor, Michigan: University Microfilms,
            1956. AC-1, #17, 595.

2.C.788.   Brzeinski, Joseph E. "Beginning Reading in Denver." The
            Reading Teacher 18(October 1974): 16-21.

2.C.789.   Buriel, Raymond. "Relationship of Three Field-Dependence
            Measures to the Reading and Math Achievement of Anglo
            American and Mexican American Children." Journal of
            Educational Psychology 70, 2(April 1978): 167-174.

2.C.790.   Cassidy, Jack. "Good News About American Education." The
            Reading Teacher 32(December 1978): 294-296.

2.C.791.   Colvin, C. R. "Methods and Materials in College Reading
            Programs. Pennsylvania Revisited, Part II." Journal
            of the Reading Specialist 7(1968): 43-49.

2.C.792.   Colvin, C. R. "Personnel in College Reading Programs.
            Pennsylvania Revisted, Part III." Journal of the
            Reading Specialist 7(1968): 90-94.

2.C.793.   Colvin, C. R. "Evaluation and Problems of College Reading
            Programs. Pennsylvania Revisited, Part IV." Journal
            of the Reading Specialist 7(1968): 139-143.

2.C.794.   Conner, Ulla. "Predictors of Second-Lnaguage Reading
            Performance." Journal of Multilingual and Multi-
            Cultural Development 4, 4(1983): 271-287.

2.C.795.   Cooper, Bernice. "An Analysis of Reading Achievement of
            White and Negro Pupils in Certain Public Schools in
            Georgia." School Review 72(Winter 1962): 462-471.

2.C.796.   Cox, Juanita, and Wallis, Beth. "Books for the Cajun
            Child--Lagniappe or a Little Something Extra for Multi-
            cultural Teaching." The Reading Teacher 36, 3(December
            1982): 263-266.

2.C.797.   Critchlow, D. E. "Johnny Does Read Better Today."
            Montana Education 42(1966): 34.

2.C.798.   Davis, Frederick B. Identification and Measurement of
            Reading Skills of High School Students. Philadelphia:
            University of Pennsylvania, 1967.

2.C.799.   Diaz, Joseph O. Perwitt. "Considerations for the Develop-
            ment of a Reading Program for Puerto Rican Bilingual
            Students." Reading Improvement 18, 4(Winter 1981):
            302-307.

2.C.800.   Downing, John. See Section 2.C.17. entry no. 302.

2.C.801.   Dummett, Leonie. "The Enigma--The Persistent Failure of
            Black Children in Learning to Read." Reading World
            24, 1(October 1984): 31-37.

2.C.802.   Elder, Richard D. See Section 2.A. entry no. 19.

2.C.803.   Farr, Robert; Fay, Leo; and Negley, Harold H. Then and
            Now: Reading Achievement in Indiana (1944-45 and
            1976). Bloomington, Indiana: Indiana University

Press, 1978.

2.C.804.   Feeley, Joan T. See Section 2.C.17. entry no. 307.

2.C.805.   Fitzgerald, Thomas P. et al. See Section 2.A. entry no.
            22.

2.C.806.   Fowler, Elaine D. "Predicting Reading Achievement of
            Spanish-Speaking First Grade Children." **Reading**
            Improvement 10, 3(Winter 1973): 7-11.

2.C.807.   Fry, Edward. See Section 2.A. entry no. 26.

2.C.808.   Furukawa, James et al. See Section 2.C.36. entry no. 573.

2.C.809.   Greaney, Vincent, et al. See Section 2.A. entry no. 30.

2.C.810.   Hagtvedt, G. A. See Section 2.C.48. entry no. 667.

2.C.811.   Hernandez, A. J. "Teaching of Reading in Puerto Rico."
            The Reading Teacher 16, (December 1962): 182-186.

2.C.812.   Hester, K. B. "Puerto Rico, Leader in a Spanish-American
            Reading Program." **The Reading Teacher** 17, (April
            1964): 516-521.

2.C.813.   Hitchcock, Dale C., and Pinder, Glenn D.   **Reading and**
            Arithmetic Achievement Among Youths 12-17 Years, as
            Measured by the Wide Range Achievement Test, United
            States; Findings from the Reading and Arithmetic Sub-
            sets of the Wide Range Achievement Test, Administered
            in a National Survey of Youths in 1966-1970.
            Rockville, Maryland: National Center for Health
            Statistics, 1974.

2.C.814.   Hughes, Theone. See Section 2.C.17. entry no. 342.

2.C.815.   Husen, Torsten. See Section 2.A. entry no. 40.

2.C.816.   Isaac, Stephen. "A Statewide Study of ECE and Non-ECE
            Schools on Reading Achievement, Grades Two and Three,
            Based on the California Assessment Program Results."
            Studies in Educational Evaluation 3(Winter 1977):
            179-194.

2.C.817.   Johnson, Lynne M.   **South Carolina First Grade Pilot**
            Project, 1975-76: The Effects of Class Size on
            Reading and Mathematics Achievement. Columbia, South
            Carolina: South Carolina Department of Education,
            1977.

2.C.818.   Johnson, Terry D. See Section 2.C.17. entry no. 348.

2.C.819.   Kalamazoo, Michigan. Board of Education. Committee to
            Study Sex Discrimination in the Kalamazoo Public
            Schools. **Sex Discrimination in an Elementary Reading**

Program: A Report Based on the Work of the Committee to Study Sex Discrimination in the Kalamazoo Public Schools. Lansing, Michigan: Michigan Women's Commission, 1974.

2.C.820. Kawakami, A. J., and Au, K. H-P. "Encouraging Reading and Language Development in Cultural Minority Children." Topics in Language Disorders 6, (March 1986): 71-80.

2.C.821. Kilty, Ted K. A Study of the Characteristics of Reading Programs in Federal, State and City-County Penal Institutions. Kalamazoo, Michigan: College of Education, Western Michigan University, 1977.

2.C.822. Kinzer, Charles K., and Stone, Ruth J. "A Comparative Study of Educators' Perceptions and use of Mandated Reading Assessments." Reading Horizons 24, 1(Fall 1983): 64-68.

2.C.823. Kirsch, Dorothy I. Sexism at Six and Seven—as Reflected in the Reading Interests of the Very Young. Paper presented at the Annual Meeting of the International Reading Association World Congress on Reading. Singapore: n.p., 1976. ED 137 723.

2.C.824. Kramer, K. See Section 2.C.44. entry no. 638.

2.C.825. Labov, William, and Robins, Clarence. "A Note on the Relation of Reading Failure to Peer Group Status in Urban Ghettos." Teachers College Record 70, 5 (February 1969): 395-405.

2.C.826. Lachat, Mary Ann, ed. Reading Programs That Work: A National Survey. Trenton, New Jersey: Office of Program Development, New Jersey State Department of Education, 1975.

2.C.827. Lapp, Diane, and Tierney, Robert J. "Reading Scores of American Nine Year Olds: NAEP's Tests." The Reading Teacher 30(April 1977): 756-760.

2.C.828. Lazar, May, ed. A Practical Guide to Individualized Reading. New York: BOE Publication No. 40, Bureau of Educational Research, 1960.

2.C.829. LeGrand, Kathryn R. "Perspective on Minority Education: An Interview with Anthropologist John Osbu." Journal of Reading 24, 8(May 1981): 680-686.

2.C.830. Lietwiler, Helena Keehne. "A Descriptive Study of Reading Programs and Practices in Public High Schools in the United States." Doctoral Dissertation, George Washington University, 1967. Dissertation Abstracts, No. 10, 3895-A.

2.C.831.   Lindgren, Scott D., et al. See Section 2.A. entry no. 63.

2.C.832.   List, L. "Remedial Reading in the Virgin Island." **Reading Improvement** 8, (Spring 1971): 16-17.

2.C.833.   Lloyd, B. A. et al. See Section 2.A. entry no. 64.

2.C.834.   Martin, W. R. "A New Look at Secondary School Reading Programs in the Upper Midwest." **Journal of Reading** 12 (1969): 467-470, 512-513.

2.C.835.   Micklos, John, Jr. "A Look at Reading Achievement in the United States: The Latest Data." **Journal of Reading** 25, 8(May 1982): 760-762.

2.C.836.   Nachman, Leonard: Getson, Russell; and Odgers, John. **Pilot Study of Ohio High School Dropouts, 1961-1962.** Columbus, Ohio: State Department of Education, 1963.

2.C.837.   Nance, A. D. "Teaching English to Speakers of Other Languages: Problems in California." In **On Teaching English to Speakers of Other Languages**, pp. 33-37. Champaign, Illinois: NCTE, 1965.

2.C.838.   National Advisory Committee on Dyslexia and Related Reading Disorders. **Reading Disorders in the United States.** Washington, D.C.: Department of Health, Education and Welfare, August 1969.

2.C.839.   National School Public Relations Association. "Compensatory Education Working, New Reading Assessment Shows." **Education USA** 23(May 4, 1981): 281, 288.

2.C.840.   National School Public Relations Association. "New York Test Scores Exceed National Average." **Education USA** 23(June 8, 1981): 322.

2.C.841.   National School Public Relations Association. "Boston Students Latest to Raise Reading Scores." **Education USA** 23(June 29, 1981): 340.

2.C.842.   National School Public Relations Association. "Scores Up Because of Hard Work, Big City School Administrators Say." **Education USA** 23(July 6, 1981): 345, 350.

2.C.843.   National Society for the Study of Education. See Section 2.A. entry no. 73.

2.C.844.   Negin, G. A. "An Effective Reading Program in a Rural Setting." **Phi Delta Kappan** 67, (January 1986): 398-399.

2.C.845.   Nevo, B., and Oren, C. "Concurrent Validity of the American Scholastic Aptitude Test (SAT) and the Israeli Inter-University Psychometric Entrance Test (IUPET).

Educational and Psychological Measurement 46, 3(Autumn 1986):   723-725

2.C.846.   Oller, John W., Jr., and Tullius, James R. "Reading Skills of Non-Native Speakers of English." International Review of Applied Linguistics in Language Teaching 11, 1(February 1973):   69-80.

2.C.847.   Oney, Bann, and Goldman, Susan R. "Decoding and Comprehensive Skills in Turkish and English: Effects of the Regularity of Grapheme-Phoneme Correspondences." Journal of Educational Psychology 76, 4(August 1984): 557-568.

2.C.848.   Oregon. Department of Education. Impact of Oregon Education: An Assessment of Reading, 1975: Oregon Statewide Assessment Program: Executive Summary. Salem, Oregon: Oregon Department of Education, 1975.

2.C.849.   Penney, Monte, and Hjelm, Howard F. "The Targeted Research and Development Program on Reading--Part I. History of the U.S. Office of Education's Support of Reading Research." American Educational Research Journal 7(May 1970):   425-434.

2.C.850.   Penty, Ruth. Reading Ability and High School Dropouts. New York: Bureau of Publications, Teachers College, Columbia University, 1956.

2.C.851.   Personke, C. See Section 2.C.55. entry no. 700.

2.C.852.   Peterson, Raymond P. See Section 2.C.17. entry no. 367.

2.C.853.   Pitts, James P. "Self-Direction and the Political Socialization of Black Youth." Social Science Quarterly 56, 1(June 1975):   93-104.

2.C.854.   Powell, William R. "The Joplin Plan: An Evaluation." Elementary School Journal 64(April 1964):   387-393.

2.C.855.   Preston, R. C. See Section 2.C.23. entry no. 459.

2.C.856.   Preston, R. C. "Comparison of Word-Recognition Skill in German and in American Children." Elementary School Journal 53, (April 1953):   443-446.

2.C.857.   Purves, Alan C. "The Potential and Real Achievement of U.S. Students in School Reading." American Journal of Education 93, 1(November 1984):   82-106.

2.C.858.   Purves, Alan C., et al. See Section 2.A. entry no. 82.

2.C.859.   Reading Programs and Practices in Elementary and Secondary Schools in Arizona. Tempe, Arizona: Bureau of Educational Research and Services, College of Education, Arizona State University, 1965.

2.C.860.   Reid, Hale C., and Beltramo, Louise. The Effect of
            Different Approaches of Initial Instruction on the
            Reading Achievement of a Selection Group of First
            Grade Children. Cedar Rapids, Iowa: Cedar Rapids
            Community School District and State University of
            Iowa, 1965.

2.C.861.   Robinson, H. M. See Section 2.C.23. entry no. 466.

2.C.862.   Rozin, P.; Poritsky, S.; and Sotsky, R. "American
            Children with Reading Problems Can Easily Learn to
            Read English Represented by Chinese Characters."
            Science 171(1971): 1264-1267. (Follow-up on July
            16, 1971).

2.C.863.   Schofer, Gil. See Section 2.C.17. entry no. 376.

2.C.864.   Scholl, Geraldine T. See Section 2.C.17. entry no. 377.

2.C.865.   Schwartz, R., et al. See Section 2.C.23. entry no. 470.

2.C.866.   Shafer, Robert E. See Section 2.C.17. entry no. 380.

2.C.867.   Sheldon, William D. "Reading Instruction in Junior High
            School." In Development in and Through Reading, 60th
            Yearbook of the NSSE, Part I, pp. 305-319. Edited by
            Paul A. Witty. Chicago: University of Chicago, 1961.

2.C.868.   Slepack, Donna Grund. See Section 2.C.22. entry no. 433.

2.C.869.   Smith, Nila Banton. American Reading Instruction. New
            York: Silver Burdett, 1934. 2nd Revised Edition,
            Newark, Delaware: International Reading Association,
            1965.

2.C.870.   Smith, Nila Banton. American Reading Instruction; Its
            Development and Its Significance in Gaining A
            Perspective on Current Practices in Reading. Newark,
            Delaware: International Reading Association, 1965.

2.C.871.   Spitzer, Rosina. See Section 2.C.17. entry no. 386.

2.C.872.   Stachelek, Deborah Ann. See Section 2.C.9. entry no. 215.

2.C.873.   Stevenson, Harold W., et al. See Section 2.A. entry no. 92.

2.C.874.   Sullivan, Joanna. "Differences in the Oral Reading Per-
            formance of English and Spanish Speaking Pupils from
            the United States and Venezuela." Journal of Research
            and Development in Education 19(Summer 1986): 68-73.

2.C.875.   Tarnopol, Lester, and Tarnopol, Muriel. "Reading and
            Learning Disabilities in the United States (with an
            emphasis on California)." In Reading Disabilities: An
            International Perspective, pp. 287-325. Edited by
            Lester Tarnopol and Muriel Tarnopol. Baltimore,

Maryland: University Park Press, 1976.

2.C.876.   Tuinmann, Jaap, et al. "Reading Achievement in the United
            States: Then and Now." Journal of Reading 19, 6
            (March 1976): 455–463.

2.C.877.   Tyler, Ralph W. See Section 2.A. entry no. 102.

2.C.878.   Whitmore, P., and Chapman, P. Dropout Incidence and
            Significance at Modesto High Schools, 1961–64.
            Modesto, California: Modesto Public Schools, 1965.

2.C.879.   Wolf, Willavene; Huck, Charlotte S; and King, Martha L.
            Critical Reading Ability of Elementary School
            Children, USOE Cooperative Research Project No. 5–
            1040. Columbus, Ohio: Research Foundation, Ohio
            State University, 1967.

2.C.880.   Wright, Esmond. See Section 2.C.17. entry no. 391.

2.C.881.   Yule, Valerie. "A Complement to Bullock: The American
            Report 'Becoming a Nation of Readers'." Reading 20,
            2(July 1986): 82–88.

2.C.882.   Ziros, Gail I. "Language Interference and Teaching the
            Chicano to Read." Journal of Reading 19, 4(January
            1976): 284–288.

        70. Uruguay

2.C.883.   Carbonell de Grompone, Maria A., et al. Estudio
            Comparativo de Los Metodos Analiticosintetico y Global
            En El Aprendizaje De La Lectura. (Comparative Study
            of the Analytic–Synthetic and Global Methods in the
            Teaching of Reading). N.P.: Published by the
            Sociedad De Dislexia Del Uruguay (Uruguyan Association
            for Dyslexia), 1967.

        71. Venezuela

2.C.884.   Sullivan, Joanna. See Section 2.C.69. entry no. 874.

        72. Wales

2.C.885.   Department of Education and Science. See Section 2.C.17.
            entry no. 300.

2.C.886.   Horton, T. R. The Reading Standards of Children in Wales.
            Bootle, Lancs: John Gardner, 1973.

2.C.887.   Start, K. B., et al. See Section 2.C.17. entry no. 387.

73. West Indies

2.C.888.   Cecil, Nancy Lee. "Impact of Interests on the Literal
            Comprehension of Beginning Readers--A West Indian
            Study." The Reading Teacher 37, 8(April 1984): 750-
            753.

2.C.889.   Driver, Geoffrey. "How West Indians Do Better at School
            (Especially the Girls)." New Society 51(January
            1980): 111-114.

2.C.890.   Edwards, V. K. "Effects of Dialect on the Comprehension
            of West Indian Children." Educational Research 18,
            2(February 1976): 83-95.

2.C.891.   Pumfrey, Peter D. See Section 2.C.17 entry no. 372.

74. Yugoslavia

2.C.892.   The Educational System of Yugoslavia. Washington, D.C.:
            Institute of International Studies (DHEW/OE), Report
            No.-DHEW-OE-75-19113. ED 104 743.

75. Zaire

2.C.893.   Biniakunu, D. D.   "Learning to Read Kikongo: A Primer
            Makes a Difference." The Reading Teacher 34, (October
            1980): 32-36.

2.C.894.   Biniakunu, D. D. "Inservice Teacher Training Improves
            Eighth Graders' Reading Ability in Zaire." Journal of
            Reading 25, 7(April 1982): 662-665.

76. Zambia

2.C.895.   Muyangana, Gideon M. Investigation of Effects of Some
            Selected Methods for Improving the Performance of Slow
            Readers in Zambian Schools. N.P., 1980.

77. Zimbabwe

2.C.896.   Hall, Harry H. "Remedial Education in Rhodesia." In
            Reading Disabilities: An International Perspective,
            pp. 265-267. Edited by Lester Tarnopol and Muriel
            Tarnopol. Baltimore, Maryland: University Park
            Press, 1976.

3

Correlates of Comparison

3.897. Aaron, Robert L., and Anderson, Martha K. "A Comparison of Values Expressed in Junvenile Magazines and Basal Reader Series." The Reading Teacher 35, 3(December 1981): 305-313.

3.898. Aaronson, Doris, et. al. See Section 4.A. entry no. 1169.

3.899. Abiri, J. O. O. See Section 2.C.46. entry no. 650.

3.900. Acland, Henry. See Section 2.C.69. entry no. 773.

3.901. Adeniran, A., et al. See Section 2.C.46. entry no. 653.

3.902. Ahmann, J. Stanley. "Differential Changes in Levels of Achievement for Students in Three Age Groups." Educational Studies 10(Spring 1979): 35-51.

3.903. "The Alphabetic Principle in Hebrew and German Constrasted to the Alphabetic Principle in English. See Section 2.C.23. entry no. 434.

3.904. Anderson, Irving H., et al. See Section 2.C.17. entry no. 273.

3.905. Anweiler, Oskar. See Section 2.B.7. entry no. 129.

3.906. Arnold, Richard D., and Sherry, Natalie. "A Comparison of the Reading Levels of Disabled Readers with Assigned Textbooks." Reading Improvement 12, 4(Winter 1975): 207-211.

3.907. August, Diane L., et al. "Comparison of Comprehension Monitoring of Skilled and Less Skilled Readers." Reading Research Quarterly 20, 1(Fall 1984): 39-53.

3.908. Austin, Gilbert, and Postlethwaite, Neville T. "Cognitive Results Based on Different Ages of Entry to School:

A Comparative Study." Journal of Educational
Psychology 66, 6(December 1974):   857–863.

3.909.   Barnitz, John G. Interrelationship of Orthography and
Phonological Structure in Learning to Read. Technical
Report No. 57. Cambridge, Massachusetts and Urbana,
Illinois: Bolt, Beranek and Newman, Inc., and
Illinois University Center for the Study of Reading,
1978. ED 150 546.

3.910.   Bear, David Eli. A Comparison of a Synthetic with an
Analytic Method of Teaching Phonics in First Grade.
Ann Arbor, Michigan: University Microfilms, 1958.
AC-1, 58–3782.

3.911.   Berger, A. See Section 2.C.9. entry no. 205.

3.912.   Berstecher, Dieter, and Dieckmann, Bernhard. "On the Role
of Comparisons in Educational Research." Comparative
Education Review 13, 1(February 1969):   96–103.

3.913.   Bjorklund, David F., and Bernholtz, Jean. "The Role of
Knowledge Base in the Memory Performance of Good and
Poor Readers." Journal of Experimental Child
Psychology 41, 2(April 1986):   367–393.

3.914.   Blachowicz, Camille L. Z. "Semantic Integration: A
Comparison of Normal and Disabled Readers." Language
and Speech 23, 2(April–June 1980):   149–158.

3.915.   Bloom, Benjamin S. Cross National Study of Educational
Attainment: Stage One of the IEA Investigation in Six
Subject Areas. Washington, D.C.: Department of
Health, Education and Welfare, Office of Education.
Final Report Project No. 6 - 2527, Grant No. HEW-OEG-
3-6-062527-2226, 1969.

3.916.   Bremer, Neville Hasso. See Section 2.C.69. entry no. 787.

3.917.   Brignac, Burke, and Wallace, Deborach S. "Palo Alto
Reading Program Versus Basics in Reading Program:
Implications for Learning Disabled." Reading Improve-
ment 19, 3(Fall 1982):   244–248.

3.918.   Brimer, M. A. "Sex Differences in Listening Comprehension." Journal of Research and Development in
Education 3(1969):   72–79.

3.919.   Bristow, Page Simpson, et al. "A Comparison of Five
Estimates of Reading Instruction Level." The Reading
Teacher 37, 3(December 1983):   273–279.

3.920.   Browning, Ellen R. "Influencing Reading Ability with
Schizophrenic Twins in Group vs. Individual Training."
Reading Improvement 11, 1(Spring 1974):   9–16.

3.921.   Bruneau, O. J. "Comparing the Reading Interest and Compre-
              hension of Fifth Grade Students." **Reading Improvement**
              23, (Summer 1986): 100-102.

3.922.   Brutten, G. J., et al. "Eye Movements of Stuttering and
              Nonstuttering Children During Silent Reading." **Journal
              of Speech and Hearing Research** 27, 4(December 1984):
              562-566.

3.923.   Bulcock, Jeffrey W., et al. See Section 2.A. entry no. 2.

3.924.   Calhoun, Calfey C., and Horner, Barbara. "Readability of
              First-Year Bookkeeping Texts Compared with Students'
              Reading Level." **Business Education Forum** 30, 1
              (October 1975): 20-21.

3.925.   Carbo, Marie. "Reading Styles Change Between Second and
              Eighth Grade." **Educational Leadership** 40, 5(February
              1983): 56-59.

3.926.   Carbonell de Grompone, Maria A., et al. See Section
              2.C.70. entry no. 883.

3.927.   Carver, Ronald P. "Measuring Reading Comprehension Using
              the Paraphrase Test and the Reading-Storage Test."
              Journal of Reading Behavior 9, 4(Winter 1977): 381-
              389.

3.928.   Chacko, Chinna. See Section 2.C.43. entry no. 634.

3.929.   Chase, Naomi Caroline. **A Comparative Study of the Word
              Recognition Abilities of Good and Poor Spellers in the
              Third Grade.** Ann Arbor, Michigan: University Micro-
              films, 1959. AC-1, 58-3519.

3.930.   Chasnoff, Robert E. **Comparision of the Intial Teaching
              Alphabet with the Traditional Alphabet in First-Grade
              Reading.** New York: McGraw-Hill, 1967.

3.931.   Chimilar, P.; Kendall, J.; and Obadia, A. **A Comparison of
              the Reading Skills of Grade One Students in French
              Immersion and Regular Classrooms.** Vancouver:
              Educational Research Institute of British Columbia,
              1984.

3.932.   Chu, Yu-Kuang. See Section 2.C.36. entry no. 571.

3.933.   Clay, Marie. See Section 2.C.45. entry no. 641.

3.934.   Cooper, Bernice. See Section 2.C.69. entry no. 795.

3.935.   Cox, Lois M., and Wilson, Alfred P. "A Comparison of
              Academic Gains in Reading Among Mildly Learning Dis-
              abled Students in Three Program Structures." **Reading
              Improvement** 18, 2(Summer 1981): 132-137.

3.936.   Critchlow, D. E.   See Section 2.C.69. entry no. 797.

3.937.   Cummings, James.   See Section 2.A. entry no. 10.

3.938.   Cutts, Warren Gibson.   A Comparative Study of Good and
           Poor Readers at the Middle Grade Level.   Ann Arbor,
           Michigan: University Microfilms, 1956.   AC-1,
           #18,015.

3.939.   Daines, Delva, and Mason, Lynne G.   "A Comparison of
           Placement Tests and Readability Graphs."   Journal of
           Reading 15, 8(May 1972):   597-603.

3.940.   Darch, C., and Gersten, R.   "Direction Setting Activities
           in Reading Comprehension: A Comparison of Two
           Approaches."   Learning Disability Quarterly 9(Summer
           1986):   235-243.

3.941.   Davey, Beth, et al.   "Comparison of Reading Comprehension
           Task Performance for Deaf and Hearing Readers."
           Journal of Speech and Hearing Research 26, 4(December
           1983):   622-628.

3.942.   Deblock, A., et al.   "Reading Comprehension in English as a
           Foreign Language: Belgium Flemish Population II."
           Studies in Educational Evaluation 6, 1(1980):   31-46.

3.943.   Deich, Ruth F.   "Reading Time and Error Rates for Normal
           and Retarded Readers."   Perceptual and Motor Skills 32,
           3(June 1971):   689-690.

3.944.   Dinnan, James.   "A Comparison of Thorndike/Lorge and
           Carroll Prime Frequency Word Lists."   Reading Improve-
           ment 12, 1(Spring 1975):   44-46.

3.945.   Dore-Boyce, Kathleen, et al.   "Comparing Reading
           Expectancy Formulas."   The Reading Teacher 29, 1
           (October 1975):   8-14.

3.946.   Douglass, Malcolm P.   See Section 2.A. entry no. 12.

3.947.   Downing, John.   "Comparision of Failure in I.T.A. and
           T.O."   The Reading Teacher 23, 1(October 1969):   43-
           47.

3.948.   Downing, John.   See Section 2.C.17. entry no. 302.

3.949.   Downing, John.   See Section 2.A. entry no. 13.

3.950.   Downing, John.   See Section 2.A. entry no. 14.

3.951.   Dubbs, Mary Wray. "How Good Were Readers in the Good Old
           Days? Replications of Two Studies." The Reading
           Teacher 32(May 1979):   933-939.

3.952.   Duck, Greg.   See Section 2.C.3. entry no. 161.

3.953.   Duck, G. See Section 2.C.3. entry no. 160.

3.954.   Duffelmyer, Frederick. "A Comparison of Average Readers
          at Different Grade Levels." Reading Horizons 21,
          2 (Winter 1981): 143-146.

3.955.   Duffelmyer, Frederick A. "A Comparison of Reading Test
          Results in Grades Nine and Twelve." Journal of Read-
          ing 23(April 1980): 606-608.

3.956.   Duffelmyer, Frederick A. "A Comparison of Two Non-compu-
          tational Readability Techniques." The Reading Teacher
          36, 1(October 1982): 4-7.

3.957.   Dunn, Lloyd M. Studies of Reading and Arithmetic in
          Mentally Retarded Boys. I A Comparision of the Read-
          Processes of Mentally Retarded and Normal Boys of the
          Same Mental Age. Lafayette, Indiana: Child Develop-
          ment Publications, 1956.

3.958.   Dwyer, C. A. "Children's Sex Role Standards and Sex Role
          Identification and Their Relationship to Achievement."
          Doctoral Dissertation, University of California at
          Berkeley, 1972.

3.959.   Dwyer, Carol Anne. "Comparative Aspects of Sex
          Differences in Reading." In Reading: What of the
          Future? pp. 267-273. Edited by Donald Moyle.
          London: United Kingdom Reading Association, 1975.

3.960.   Dwyer, Edward J. "Analysis of Reading Achievement, Listen-
          ing Comprehension and Paradigmatic Language of Selected
          Second Grade Students by Race and Sex." Southern
          Journal of Educational Research 14, 3(Summer 1980):
          205-218.

3.961.   Eeds, Maryann, and Cockrum, Ward A. "Teaching Word
          Meanings by Expanding Schemata vs. Dictionary Work vs.
          Reading in Context." Journal of Reading 28, 6(March
          1985): 492-497.

3.962.   Elgart, Denise B. "Oral Reading, Silent Reading and
          Listening Comprehension: A Comparative Study."
          Journal of Reading Behavior 10, 2(Summer 1978): 203-
          207.

3.963.   Elligett, Jane, and Tocco, Thomas S. "Reading Achievement
          in 1979 vs. Achievement in the Fifties." Phi Delta
          Kappan 61(June 1980): 698-699.

3.964.   Ellis, E. N. "Comparison of Reading Achievement in the
          Fourth Year: Initial Teaching Alphabet (I.T.A.) Versus
          Traditional Orthography (T.O.)." Vancouver: Board of
          School Trustees, Department of Research and Speical
          Services, 1970.

3.965.   Farr, Roger, and Blomenberg, Paula. "Contrary to Popular
          Opinion...Children Today Are Exhibiting Better Reading
          Skills Than Their Predecessors." Early Years 9(May
          1979): 52-53, 68.

3.966.   Farr, Robert, et al. "Scholastic Aptitude Test Performance
          and Reading Ability." Journal of Reading 28,
          3(December 1984): 208-214.

3.967.   Feldmann, Shirley, and Weiner, Max. "The Use of a
          Standardized Reading Achievement Test with Two Levels
          of Socio-Economic Status Pupils." Journal of Experi-
          mental Education 32(Spring 1964): 269-274.

3.968.   Field, Helen Atwater. Extensive Individual Reading Versus
          Class Reading; a Study of the Development of Reading
          in the Transition Grades. New York: Bureau of
          Publications, Teachers College, Columbia University,
          1930. (New York: AMS Press, 1972).

3.969.   Fisher, Dennis F., and Frankfurter, Anthony. "Normal and
          Disabled Readers Can Locate and Identify Letters:
          Where's the Perceptual Deficit?" Journal of Reading
          Behavior 9, 1(Spring 1977): 31-43.

3.970.   Fitzgerald, Thomas P., et al. See Section 2.A. entry
          no. 22.

3.971.   Foster, Marion E., et al. See Section 2.C.9. entry no.
          206.

3.972.   Fowler, William. "A Study of Process and Method in Three-
          Year-Old Twins and Triplets Learning to Read."
          Genetic Psychology Monographs 72(1965): 3-89.

3.973.   Fry, Edward Bernard. First Grade Reading Instruction
          Using a Diacritical Marking System. The Initial
          Teaching Alphabet and A Basal Reading System. New
          Brunswick, New Jersey: Rutgers State University,
          1965.

3.974.   Fry, Edward. See Section 2.A. entry no. 26.

3.975.   Gates, Arthur Irving. Reading Attainment in Elementary
          Schools: 1957 and 1937. New York: Bureau of Pub-
          lications, Teachers College, Columbia University,
          1961.

3.976.   Gates, Arthur I. assisted by Batchelder, Mildred I.; and
          Betzner, Jean. "A Modern Systematic Versus an
          Opportunistic Method of Teaching: An Experimental
          Study." Teachers College Record 27(April 1926): 679-
          700.

3.977.   Gee, Thomas Carroll, et al. "A Comparison of Reading
          Comprehension Across Selection Content Areas."

Reading Psychology 6, 3-4(1985):   223-230.

3.978.   Gillen, Barry, et al.   "Reading Ease and Human Interest
              Scores: A Comparison of Flesch Scores with Subjective
              Ratings." Teaching of Psychology 4, 1(February 1977):

3.979.   Gold, J. and Fleisher, L. S.   "Comprehension Breakdown with
              Inductively Organized Text: Differences Between
              Average and Disabled Readers." Remedial and Special
              Education 7(July/August 1986):   26-32.

3.980.   Goodacre, Elizabeth J., et al.   See Section 2.C.17. entry
              no. 324.

3.981.   Graham, Steve.   "Comparing the SQ3R Method with Other
              Study Techniques for Reading Improvement." Reading
              Improvement 19, 1(Spring 1982):   45-47.

3.982.   Granzow, Kent Rayburn. A Comparative Study of Under-
              Achievers, Normal Achievers, and Overachievers in
              Reading. Ann Arbor, Michigan: University Microfilms,
              1954. AC-1, #7563.

3.983.   Greaney, Vincent. See Section 2.C.32. entry no. 521.

3.984.   Greaney, Vincent, and Clarke, Michael.   "A Longitudinal
              Study of Two Reading Methods on Leisure Time Reading
              Habits." In Reading: What of the Future?, pp. 107-
              114. Edited by Donald Moyle. London: United Kingdom
              Reading Association, 1975.

3.985.   Great Britain. See Section 2.C.17. entry no. 328.

3.986.   Great Britain. See Section 2.C.17. entry no. 329.

3.987.   Great Britain. See Section 2.C.17. entry no. 330.

3.988.   Groebel, Lillian. See Section 2.C.17 entry no. 332.

3.989.   Grundin, Hans U., et al. See Section 2.A. entry no. 32.

3.990.   Guidry, Loyd J., and Knight, D. Frances.   "Comparative
              Readability: Four Formulas and Newberg Books."
              Journal of Reading 19, 7(April 1976):   552-556.

3.991.   Guthrie, John T.   "Learnability Versus Readability of
              Texts." Journal of Educational Research 65,
              2(February 1972): 273-280.

3.992.   Hagtvedt, G. A. See Section 2.C.48. entry no. 667.

3.993.   Hahn, Robert B. A Study of the Relative Effectiveness of
              Three Methods of Teaching Reading in Grade One.
              Pontiac, Michigan: Oakland Schools, 1965.

3.994.   Harber, Jean R. "The Effects of Illustrations on the Read-
            ing Performance of Learning Disabled and Normal
            Children." **Learning Disability Quarterly** 6, 1(Winter
            1983):   55-60.

3.995.   Harper, J. A., and Ewing, N. J. "A Comparison of the
            Effectiveness of Microcomputer and Workbook Instruction
            on Reading Comprehension Performance of High Incidence
            Handicapped Children." **Educational Technology** 26,
            (May 1986):   40-45.

3.996.   Harris, Albert J., and Jacobson, Milton D. "Some
            Comparisons Between Basic Elementary Reading Vocabu-
            laries and Other Word Lists." **Reading Research
            Quarterly** 9, 1(Fall 1973-1974):   87-109.

3.997.   Harris, Albert J., and Serwer, Blanche L. **Comparisons of
            Reading Approaches in First Grade Teaching with Dis-
            advantaged Children.** New York: Office of Research
            and Evaluation, Division of Teacher Evaluation, City
            University of New York, USOE Cooperative Research
            Project No. 2677, 1966.

3.998.   Harris, Albert J.; Serwer, Blanche L.; and Gold, Lawrence.
            "Comparing Reading Approaches in First Grade Teaching
            with Disadvantaged Children Extended into Second
            Grade." **The Reading Teacher** 20(May 1967):   698-703.

3.999.   Hartlep, Karen L., and Dolan, Ellen. "A Comparison of
            Readers Versus Non-Readers in a Cognitive Synthesis
            Task." **Journal of Reading Behavior** 12, 3(Fall 1980):
            237-241.

3.1000.   Heerman, Charles E., and Sheen, Sy-yng Violet. "Reading
            Gains of Traditional and Non-Traditional Students."
            Paper presented at the Annual Meeting of the Plains
            Regional Conference of the International Reading
            Association. Wichita, Kansas: 1983.   ED 236 554.

3.1001.   Heideman, Paul John. **A Study of the Relationship Between
            Televiewing and Reading Abilities of Eighth Grade
            Students.** Ann Arbor: University Microfilms, 1957.
            AC-1, #22, 457.

3.1002.   Hill, Walter Raymond. **A Multivariate Comparison of College
            Freshman with Adequate or Deficient Reading Comprehen-
            sion.** Ann Arbor, Michigan: University Microfilm,
            1959.   AC-1, 58-5829.

3.1003.   Hitchcock, Dale C., et al. See Section 2.C.69. entry
            no. 813.

3.1004.   Holmes, Betty C., and Allison, Ray W. "The Effect of Far
            Modes of Reading on Children's Comprehension." **Read-
            ing Research and Instruction** 25, 1(Fall 1985):   9-20.

3.1005.   Hood, Joyce, et al. See Section 2.A. entry no. 36.

3.1006.   Ho, Wai-Ching, and Eiszler, Charles F. **Interaction**
            Effects of Socio-economic Status, Intelligence and
            Reading Program on Beginning Reading Achievement.
            Paper presented at the Meeting of the American
            Educational Research Association. Minneapolis: n.p.,
            1970. ED 039 114.

3.1007.   Horner, J., et al. See Section 2.C.3 entry no. 167.

3.1008.   Hunter, William J., et al. See Section 2.C.9 entry no. 212.

3.1009.   Husen, Torsten. See Section 2.A. entry no. 37.

3.1010.   Husen, Torsten. See Section 2.A. entry no. 38.

3.1011.   Husen, Torsten. See Section 2.A. entry no. 40.

3.1012.   International Association for the Evaluation of
            Educational Achievement. See Section 2.A. entry no.
            41.

3.1013.   International Association for the Evaluation of
            Educational Achievement. See Section 2.A. entry no.
            42.

3.1014.   International Association for the Evaluation of
            Educational Achievement. See Section 2.A. entry no.
            43.

3.1015.   International Association for the Evaluation of
            Educational Achievement. See Section 2.A. entry no.
            44.

3.1016.   International Association for the Evaluation of
            Educational Achievement. See Section 2.A. entry no.
            45.

3.1017.   International Association for the Evaluation of
            Educational Achievement. See Section 2.A. entry no.
            46.

3.1018.   Johns, Jerry L. "Some Comparisons Between the Dolch Basic
            Sight Vocabulary and the Word List for the 1970's."
            Reading World 15, 3(March 1976): 144-150.

3.1019.   Johns, Jerry L. "Equivalence of Forms 1 and 3, Level E,
            Gates-MacGinitie Reading Tests." **Journal of Reading**
            28, 1(October 1984): 48-51.

3.1020.   Johnson, Dale D. See Section 2.A. entry no. 49.

3.1021.   Johnson, Dale D. See Section 2.A. entry no. 50.

3.1022.   Johnson, Joseph C., II. "Some Aspects of Two Noncon-

ventional Reading Programs." International Reading
Association Conference Proceedings, Part 1, 13(April
1968): 341-347.

3.1023.   Johnson, Lynne M. See Section 2.C.69. entry no. 817.

3.1024.   Johnson, Marjorie S., and Kress, Roy A. Informal Reading
Inventories. Newark, Delaware: International Reading
Association, 1965.

3.1025.   Karlsen, Bjorn. A Comparison of Some Educational and
Psychological Characteristics of Successful and Un-
Successful Readers at the Elementary School Level.
Ann Arbor, Michigan: University Microfilms, 1955.
Ac-1, #11,095.

3.1026.   Kendrick, William M., and Bennett, Clayton L.
"Comparative Study of Two First Grade Language Arts
Programs." Reading Research Quarterly II, 1(Fall
1966): 83-118.

3.1027.   Khokhlova, W. See Section 2.C.62. entry no. 732.

3.1028.   Kincaid, J. Peter, and Gamble, Louis G. "Ease of Comprehension of Standard and Readable Automobile Insurance
Policies as a Function of Reading Ability." Journal
of Reading Behavior 9, 1(Spring 1977): 85-87.

3.1029.   Kinzer, Charles K., et al. See Section 2.C.69 entry no. 822.

3.1030.   Kirkland, Eleanor R. "The Effect of Two Different Orthographies on Beginning Reading." International Reading
Association Conference Proceedings, Part 1, 13(April
1968): 664-671.

3.1031.   Kleist, K. "Introduction: Contemporary Schools of
Psychiatry, Wernicke and Cerebral Localizers." In
Clinical Psychiatry, 3rd Edition. Edited by W. Mayer-
Gross, E. Slater, and M. Roth. London: Bailliere,
Tendall and Cassell, 1969.

3.1032.   Klemish, Janice J. "A Comparison Study of Two Methods of
Teaching Music Reading to First Grade Children."
Journal of Research in Music Education 18, 4(Winter
1970): 355-364.

3.1033.   Kline, Carl L., et al. See Section 2.C.28. entry no. 491.

3.1034.   Kline, Carl L., et al. See Section 2.A. entry no. 58.

3.1035.   Klumb, Roger William. The Effects of Monitoring Pupil
Performance and Two Incentive Treatments for Teachers
on Pupils' Reading Skill Development and Teachers'
Attitudes. Madison, Wisconsin: Research and Develop-
ment Center for Cognitive Learning, University of
Wisconsin, 1973.

3.1036.   Kramer, K.   See Section 2.C.44. entry no. 638.

3.1037.   Kugelmass, S., et al.   See Section 2.A. entry no. 60.

3.1038.   Kumar, Krishna. Literature in the Reading Textbook: A
           Comparative Study from a Sociological Perspective.
           Toronto: University of Toronto, Reading Series
           Analysis, 1980.   ED 204 706.

3.1039.   Kurzman, Maurice. "The Reading Ability of College Fresh-
           men Compared to the Readability of Their Textbooks."
           Reading Improvement 11, 2(Fall 1974): 13-25.

3.1040.   Kyostio, O. K.   See Section 2.C.20 entry no. 397.

3.1041.   Lapp, Diane, et al.   See Section 2.C.69. entry no. 827.

3.1042.   Latham, Dorothy. Six Reading Schemes: Their Emphases and
           Their Interchangeability. Cambridge (Shaftesbury
           Road, Cambridge): Cambridge Institute of Education,
           1971.

3.1043.   Lefton, Lester A., et al. "Eye Movements in Reading
           Disabled and Normal Children: A Study of Systems and
           Strategies." Journal of Learning Disabilities 11,
           9(November 1978): 559-566.

3.1044.   Legrand, Louis. See Section 2.A. entry no. 62.

3.1045.   Lewy, Arieh. See Section 2.C.33 entry no. 560.

3.1046.   Lietwiler, Helena Keehne. See Section 2.C.69. entry no.
           830.

3.1047.   Lindsay, Geoff; Evans, Alison; and Jones, Ben. "Paired
           Reading Versus Relaxed Reading: A Comparison."
           British Journal of Educational Psychology 55, 3
           (November 1985): 304-309.

3.1048.   Lloyd, B. A., et al. See Section 2.A. entry no. 64.

3.1049.   Lobban, G. "Sex Roles in Reading Schemes." Educational
           Research 27, (June 1975): 202-210.

3.1050.   MacNamara, John. "Comparative Studies of Reading and
           Problem Solving in Two Languages." TESOL Quarterly
           4, 2(June 1970): 107-116.

3.1051.   Maminta, Rosario E. See Section 2.C.52. entry no. 685.

3.1052.   Manning, Maryann M., and Manning, Gary L. "Early Readers
           and Nonreaders from Low Socioeconomic Environments:
           What Their Parents Report." The Reading Teacher; 38,
           1(October 1984): 32-34.

3.1053.   Marita, Sister. A Comparative Study of Beginning Reading
           Achievement Under Three Classroom Organizational
           Patterns: Modified Individualized, Three-to-Five
           Groups, and Whole-Class, Language-Experience.
           Milwaukee, Wisconsin: Marquette University, 1965.

3.1054.   Marklund, Sixten. See Section 2.C.63. entry no. 760.

3.1055.   Maxwell, Madeline M. See Section 4.A. entry no. 1206.

3.1056.   Mayes, Paul B. "A Comparison of the Readability of
           Synopses and Original Articles for Engineering
           Synopses." Journal of the American Society for
           Information Science 29, 6(November 1978): 312-313.

3.1057.   McCall, Rozanne A., and McCall, Robert B. "Comparative
           Validity of Five Reading Diagnostic Tests." Journal
           of Eductational Research 62, 7(March 1969): 323-328.

3.1058.   McCullough, Constance M. et al. See Section 2.A. entry
           no. 71.

3.1059.   McDonagh, D. See Section 2.C.32. entry no. 530.

3.1060.   McDonagh, Declan. See Section 2.C.32. entry no. 531.

3.1061.   Miller, Gloria E. "The Effects of General and Specific
           Self-Instruction on Children's Comprehension Monitoring
           Performances During Reading." Reading Research
           Quarterly 20, 5(Fall 1985): 616-628.

3.1062.   Modiano, Nancy. "National or Mother Language in Beginning
           Reading: A Comparative Study." Research in the
           Teaching of English 2(Spring 1968): 32-43.

3.1063.   Moore, Dennis W., et al. See Section 2.C.50. entry no. 677.

3.1064.   Moorhouse, A. J., and Yule, William. "A Comparison of the
           Neale and the Daniels and Diack Reading Tests."
           Reading 8, 3(December 1974): 24-27.

3.1065.   Mycock, M. See Section 2.C.17. entry no. 363.

3.1066.   National Assessment of Educational Progress. Reading,
           Thinking and Writing: Results from the 1979-1980
           National Assessment of Reading and Literature. Report
           No. 11-L-01. Denver, Colorado: National Assessment of
           Educational Progress, 1981.

3.1067.   Neville, Mary H. See Section 2.C.20. entry no. 402.

3.1068.   Neville, Mary H. See Section 2.C.59. entry no. 713.

3.1069.   Nicholas, Goldie Francis. The Relative Effectiveness of
           Two Types of Phonetic Materials on the Reading
           Achievement of Second Grade Pupils. Ann Arbor,

Michigan: University Microfilms, 1957.   AC-1,
#24, 243.

3.1070.   Nichols, Ruth.   **A Comparison of Three Group Reading Tests
in Surveying the Attainment of First Year Secondary
Children.**   Reading: Centre for the Teaching of
Reading, University of Reading School of Education,
1975.

3.1071.   Nisbet, John, et al.   See Section 2.C.55. entry no. 699.

3.1072.   Noonan, Richard D.   See Section 2.A. entry no. 74.

3.1073.   Norman, Charles A., and Malicky, Grace V.   "A Comparison of
Two Approaches for Teaching Reading to Adults."   **Adult
Literacy and Basic Education** 8, 2(1984):   91-101.

3.1074.   Oakhill, Jane; Yuill, Nicola; and Parkin, Alan.   "On the
Nature of the Difference Between Skilled and Less-
Skilled Comprehenders."   **Journal of Research in Reading**
9, 2(September 1986):   80-91.

3.1075.   Obonai, Torao, et al.   See Section 2.C.36. entry no. 586.

3.1076.   Odland, Ruby Norine.   **A Comparative Study of the Word
Recognition Abilities of Good and Poor Readers in the
Third Grade.**   Ann Arbor, Michigan: University
Microfilms, 1959.   AC-1, #58-3552.

3.1077.   Ohanian, Vera.   "Control Populations in I.T.A.
Experiments."   **Elementary English** 43(1966):   373-380.

3.1078.   Olander, Herbert T., and Ehmer, Charles L.   "What Pupils
Know About Vocabulary in Mathematics--1930 and 1968."
Elementary School Journal 71, 7(April 1971):   361-367.

3.1079.   Ollila, Lloyd O.   See Section 2.A. entry no. 75.

3.1080.   Olson, Arthur V.   "Relation of Achievement of Test Scores
and Specific Reading Abilities to the Frostig Developmental Tests of Visual Perception."   **Perceptual and
Motor Skills** 22(February 1966):   179-184.

3.1081.   Ortiz, V.   "Reading Activities and Reading Proficiency
Among Hispanic, Black and White Students."   **American
Journal of Education** 95(November 1986):   58-76.

3.1082.   Peaker, Gilbert F.   See Section 2.A. entry no. 76.

3.1083.   Peoples, Arthur C., and Nelson, Rosemary O.   "The
Differential Effects of Phonics Versus Sight-
Recognition Methods of Teaching Reading on the Eye
Movements of Good and Poor Second Grade Readers."
Journal of Reading Behavior 9, 4(Winter 1977):   327-
337.

3.1084.   Perelstein de Braslavsky, Berta. See Section 2.C.1. entry
            no. 140.

3.1085.   Perelstein de Braslavsky, Berta. See Section 2.C.1. entry
            no. 141.

3.1086.   Personke, C. See Section 2.C.55. entry no. 700.

3.1087.   Peterson, Raymond P. See Section 2.C.17. entry no. 367.

3.1088.   Pidgeon, Douglas A. See Section 2.C.3. entry no. 179.

3.1089.   Porter, D. "Six Area Studies." **Comparative Education 7,**
            1(August 1971): 15-20.

3.1090.   Postlethwaite, T. Neville. See Section 2.A. entry no. 78.

3.1091.   Postlethwaite, T. Neville. See Section 2.A. entry no. 79.

3.1092.   Postlethwaite, T. N. See Section 2.A. 80.

3.1093.   Postlethwaite, T. Neville, ed. See Section 2.A. 81.

3.1094.   Preston, R. C. See Section 2.C.23. entry no. 459.

3.1095.   Pring, Linda. "A Comparison of the Word Recognition
            Processes of Blind and Sighted Children." **Child
            Development** 55, 5(October 1984): 1865-1877.

3.1096.   Purves, Alan C., et al. **Reading and Literature: American
            Achievement in International Perspective.** Urbana,
            Illinois: National Council of Teachers of English,
            1981. ED 199 741.

3.1097.   Quorn, Kerry Charles, and Yore, Larry Dean. "Comparison
            Studies of Reading Readiness Skills Acquisition by
            Different Methods: Formal Reading Readiness Program,
            Informal Reading Readiness Program, and a Kindergarten
            Science Program." **Science Education** 62, 4(October-
            December 1978): 459-465.

3.1098.   Raban, Bridie. **Reading Skill Acquisition: Comparative
            Lists of Reading Games and Support Materials.** Read-
            ing, England: Centre for the Teaching of Reading,
            School of Education, University of Reading, 1976.

3.1099.   Ranta, T. M. See Section 2.C.20 entry no. 403.

3.1100.   Ratekin, Ned. "A Comparison of Reading Achievement Among
            Three Racial Groups Using Standard Reading Materials."
            In **Cross-Cultural Perspectives on Reading and Reading
            Research,** pp. 62-67. Edited by Dina Feitelson.
            Newark, Delaware: International Reading Association,
            1978.

3.1101.   Reid, Hale C., et al. See Section 2.C.69. entry no. 860.

3.1102.   Riding, R. J., and Hardaker, R. W. "The Effectiveness of
           an Instructional Videotape and Computer Presented
           Activities on Pre-Reading Skills with Three-Year-Old
           Children." Journal of Educational Television 12,
           1(1986): 7-17.

3.1103.   Robinson, H. Alan, et al. Expressed Reading Interests of
           Young Children: An International Study. Paper
           presented at the International Reading Association
           World Congress on Reading. Vienna: n.p., 1974. ED
           096 614.

3.1104.   Robinson, H. M. See Section 2.C.23. entry no. 466.

3.1105.   Robinson, Richard D.; Goodacre, Elizabeth J.; and McKenna,
           Michael C. "Psycholinguistic Beliefs: A Cross-
           Cultural Study of Teacher Practice." Reading Improve-
           ment 15, 2(Summer 1978): 134-157.

3.1106.   Rogers, Arnold R. "Comparing the Difficulty of Basal
           Readers." New England Reading Association Journal 5,
           2(Winter 1970): 35-37.

3.1107.   Root, Shelton L., Jr. "A Comparison of Realistic Contemp-
           orary Fiction by Non-American and American Authors for
           Children Nine Through Twelve." In Cross-Cultural
           Perspectives on Reading and Reading Research, pp. 115-
           125. Edited by Dina Feitelson. Newark, Delaware:
           International Reading Association, 1978.

3.1108.   Ruddell, Robert B. "The Effect of Four Programs of
           Reading Instruction with Varying Emphasis on the
           Regularity of Grapheme-Phoneme Correspondences and the
           Relation of Language Structure to Meaning and Achieve-
           ment in First Grade Reading." Berkeley, California:
           University of California, 1965.

3.1109.   Russell, D. R. See Section 2.C.17. entry no. 374.

3.1110.   Sabaroff, Rose E. "A Comparative Investigation of Six
           Reading Programs: Two Basal, Four Linguistic."
           Education 91, 4(April-May 1971): 303-314.

3.1111.   Schlief, Mabel, and Wood, Robert W. "A Comparison of
           Procedures to Determine Readability Level of Non-Text
           Materials." Reading Improvement 11, 2(Fall 1974):
           57-64.

3.1112.   Scholl, Geraldine T. See Section 2.C.17. entry no. 377.

3.1113.   Schwartz, R., et al. See Section 2.C.23. entry no. 470.

3.1114.   Seifert, Kelvin. "Comparison of Verbal Interaction in Two
           Preschool Programs." Young Children 24, 6(September):
           350-355.

3.1115.   Seymour, Dorothy Z. "The Difference Between Linguistics
             and Phonics." The Reading Teacher 23, 2(November
             1969): 99–102.

3.1116.   Shafer, Robert E. See Section 2.C.17. entry no. 379.

3.1117.   Shafer, Susan M. "Folklore, East and West." In Reading:
             What of the Future? pp. 274–278. Edited by Donald
             Moyle. London: United Kingdom Reading Association,
             1975.

3.1118.   Shapiro, Bernard J.; Willford, Robert E.; and Shapiro,
             Phyllis P. "The I.T.A. Transition Problem—A
             Comparative Study." Journal of Educational Research
             65, 2(October 1971): 57–60.

3.1119.   Sheldon, William D., and Lashinger, Donald R. Effect of
             First Grade Instruction Using Basal Readers, Modified
             Linguistic Materials, and Linguistic Readers.
             Syracuse, New York: Syracuse University, 1966.

3.1120.   Slepack, Donna Grund. See Section 2.C.22. entry no. 433.

3.1121.   Smith, Carl Bernard. "First Grade Composition as It
             Relates to Two Methods of Beginning Reading in Inner
             City Schools." International Reading Association
             Proceedings Part 1, 13(April 1968): 737–743.

3.1122.   Smith, Carl B. "Evaluating Title I and Innovative Read-
             ing Programs: Problems and Procedures." In Measure-
             ment and Evaluation of Reading, pp. 60–79. Edited by
             Roger Farr. New York: Harcourt, 1970.

3.1123.   Smith, Lawrence L. "Comparing Reading Expectancy Sets as
             Determined from Selected Intelligence Measures."
             Reading Improvement 12, 4(Winter 1975): 212–219.

3.1124.   Smith, Linda Cleora. A Study of Laterality Character-
             istics of Retarded Readers and Reading Achievers.
             Ann Arbor, Michigan: University Microfilms, 1954.
             AC-1, #8192.

3.1125.   Smith, Nila B. Reading Instruction for Today's Children.
             Englewood Cliffs, New Jersey: Prentice-Hall, 1965.

3.1126.   Spencer, Doris U., and Moquin, L. Doris. Individualized
             Reading Versus a Basal Reader Program at First Grade
             Level in Rural Communities. Johnson, Vermont:
             Johnson State College, 1966.

3.1127.   Spitzer, Rosina. See Section 2.C.17. entry no. 386.

3.1128.   Stallard, Cathy. "Managing Reading Instruction:
             Comparative Analysis of Objective-Based Reading
             Programs." Educational Technology 17, 12(December
             1977): 21–26.

3.1129.   Stauffer, Russell. "Do Sex Differences Affect Reading?"
           The Instructor (May 1968): 25.

3.1130.   Stauffer, Russell G., and Hammond, W. Dorsey. Effective-
           ness of a Language Arts and Basic Reader Approach to
           First Grade Reading Instruction. Newark, Delaware:
           University of Delaware, 1965.

3.1131.   Stemmler, Anne O. "Reading of Highly Creative Versus
           Highly Intelligent Secondary Students." International
           Reading Association Conference Proceedings Part 1,
           13 (April 1968): 821-831.

3.1132.   Stevenson, Robert L. See Section 2.A. entry no. 93.

3.1133.   Strickland, Dorothy S. See Section 2.A. entry no. 94.

3.1134.   Swalm, James E. "A Comparison of Oral Reading, Silent
           Reading and Listening Comprehension." Education 92,
           4(April-May 1972): 111-115.

3.1135.   Tankard, James William Jr., and Tankard, Elaine F.
           "Comparison of Readability of Basic Reporting Texts."
           Journalism Quarterly 54, 4(Winter 1977): 794-797.

3.1136.   Tarnopol, Lester, and Tarnopol, Muriel, eds. Comparative
           Reading and Learning Difficulties. Lexington:
           Massachusetts: Lexington Books, 1981.

3.1137.   Taylor, Nancy E. "The Effects of Text Manipulation and
           Multiple Reading Strategies on the Reading Performance
           of Good and Poor Readers." Reading Research Quarterly
           20, 5(Fall 1985): 566-574.

3.1138.   Thackray, Derek V. Readiness to Read with I.T.A. and T.O.
           London: Geoffrey Chapman, 1970.

3.1139.   Throndike, Robert L. See Section. 2.A. entry no. 99.

3.1140.   Thorndike, Robert L. See Section 2.A. entry no. 100.

3.1141.   Tomasi, Tina. "Reading and Work in the Public School
           During the Liberal and Fascist Period." Western
           European Education 14, 3(Fall 1982): 7-29.

3.1142.   Travers, Michael. See Section 2.C.32. entry no. 536.

3.1143.   Traynelis-Yurek, Elaine. "Preferred Versus Non-Preferred
           Hand: A Comparative Study." Academic Therapy 21, 1
           (September 1985): 29-36.

3.1144.   Tuinmann, Jaap, et al. See Section 2.C.69. entry no. 876.

3.1145.   Tyler, Ralph W. "The U.S. vs. The World: A Comparison
           of Educational Performance." Phi Delta Kappan 62,
           5(January 1981): 307-310.

3.1146.   Tzeng, O. I. L., et al. See Section 2.C.36. entry no.
           621.

3.1147.   Van Allen, Roach. **Reading Programs: Alternatives for
           Improvement.** Washington: American Association of
           Elementary-Kindergarten-Nursery Educators, 1973.

2.1148.   Vellutino, Frank R., and Scanlon, Donna M. "Free Recall of
           Concrete and Abstract Words in Poor and Normal
           Readers." **Journal of Experimental Child Psychology**
           39, 2(April 1985): 363–380.

3.1149.   Venezky, Richard L. See Section 2.C.20. entry no. 407.

3.1150.   Vilscek, Elaine C., and Cleland, Donald L. **Two Approaches
           to Reading Instruction.** Washington, D.C.: U.S.
           Office of Education, Bureau of Research, 1968.

3.1151.   Vogel, Susan Ann. **Syntactic Abilities in Normal and
           Dyslexic Children.** Baltimore: University Park Press,
           1975.

3.1152.   Walker, D.A. See Section 2.A. entry no. 104.

3.1153.   Walker, Laurence. "A Comparative Study of Selected Read-
           ing and Listening Processes." **Reading Research
           Quarterly** 10, 2(1974–1975): 255–257.

2.1154.   Ward, L. O. "Variables Influencing Auditory-Visual In-
           tegration in Normal and Retarded Readers." **Journal of
           Reading Behavior** 9, (Fall 1977): 290–295.

3.1155.   Ward, William D., and Barcher, Peter R. "Reading Achieve-
           ment and Creativity as Related to Open Classroom
           Experience." **Journal of Educational Psychology** 67,
           5(October 1975): 683–691.

3.1156.   Warren, Ann, and Coston, Frederick E. "A Comparative
           Study of Attitudes of First Grade Children in Two
           Reading Programs--Individualized and Basal." **Reading
           Horizons** 15, 4(Summer 1975): 189–197.

3.1157.   Wilberg, J. Lawrence, et al. See Section 2.A. entry no.
           106.

3.1158.   Williams, Martha Steele, and Knafle, June D. "Comparative
           Difficulty of Vowel and Consonant Sounds for Beginning
           Readers." **Reading Improvement** 14, 1(Spring 1977):
           2–10.

3.1159.   Wilson, Grace Elizabeth. **The Comparative Value of
           Different Types of Developmental Reading Programs at
           Tenth Grade Level.** Ann Arbor, Michigan: University
           Microfilms, 1956. AC-1, #16,045.

3.1160.   Wishart, Elizabeth, and Smith, J. Lea. "Understanding of

Logical Connectiveness in History." **Australian Journal of Reading** 6, 1(March 1983): 19–29.

3.1161.   World Congress on Reading, ed, Sydney, 1970. See Section 2.A. entry no. 107.

3.1162.   **World Survey of Education II.** See Section 2.A. entry no. 108.

3.1163.   **World Survey of Education III.** See Section 2.A. entry no. 109.

3.1164.   Wyatt, Nita M. "The Reading Achievement of First Grade Boys vs. First Grade Girls." **Reading Teacher** 19(May 1966): 661–665.

3.1165.   Wyatt, Nita M. **Reading Achievements of First Grade Boys Versus First Grade Girls Using Two Approaches: A Linguistic Approach and a Basal Reader Approach with Boys and Girls Grouped Separately.** Lawrence, Kansas: University of Kansas, 1965.

3.1166.   Yarmohammadi, Lotfollah. "Universal Versus Language Study-Specific Tests." **English Language Teaching Journal** 29, 1(October 1974): 65–68.

3.1167.   Yoloye, E. Ayotunde. See Section 2.B.1. entry no. 115.

3.1168.   Zirbes, Laura. **Comparative Studies of Current Practice in Reading, with Techniques for the Improvement of Teaching.** New York: Bureau of Publications, Teachers Press, 1972.

4

Correlates of Learning to Read

A. LEARNING TO READ

4.A.1169.   Aaronson, Doris, and Ferres, Steven. "Reading Strategies for Children and Adults: Some Empirical Evidence." Journal of Verbal Learning and Verbal Behavior 23, 2(April 1984): 189-220.

4.A.1170.   Ahuja, Pramila. "Helping Children Read Through Story-telling." Reading 18, 1(April 1984): 37-42.

4.A.1171.   Aranha, M. "Sustained Silent Reading Goes East." The Reading Teacher 39, (November 1985): 214-217.

4.A.1172.   Baker, Graeme. "Learning to Read: Children's Responses to the Look and Say Method." Educational Review 32, 2(June 1980): 133-150.

4.A.1173.   Barney, W. D. See Section 2.C.45. entry no. 639.

4.A.1174.   Barrett, Thomas C. "The Relationship Between Measures of Pre-Reading Visual Discrimination and First-Grade Reading Achievement: A Review of the Literature." Reading Research Quarterly 1(Fall 1965): 51-76.

4.A.1175.   Behrstock, Julian. "Books for All: International Cooperation to Promote Reading." Journal of Reading 23, 4(January 1980): 313-319.

4.A.1176.   Bond, Guy, and Dykstra, Robert. Coordinating Center for the First Grade Reading Instruction Programs. Minneapolis, Minnesota: University of Minnesota, Final Report of USOE Project 5-0341, ERIC Document No. ED 013 714, 1967.

4.A.1177.   Booth, Vera Southgate. See Section 2.C.17. entry no. 287.

4.A.1178.   Brignac, Burke, et al. See Section 3 entry no. 917.

4.A.1179.   Brogan, Peggy, and Fox, Lorene K. **Helping Children Read.**
             New York: Holt, 1961.

4.A.1180.   Brzeinsky, Joseph E. See Section 2.C.69. entry no. 788.

4.A.1181.   Cane, Brian S., and Smithers, Jane. **The Roots of Reading:**
             a Study of 12 Infant Schools in Deprived Areas.
             Slough (England): National Foundation for Educational
             Research, 1971.

4.A.1182.   Cazden, Courtney B. **Language in Early Childhood and Read-**
             ing: A Review for 1969-70. Washington, D.C.: Center
             for Applied Linguistics, ERIC Clearinghouse for
             Linguistics, 1970. ED 043 867.

4.A.1183.   Chall, J. S. **Learning to Read: The Great Debate.** New
             York: McGraw-Hill, 1967.

4.A.1184.   Chasnoff, Robert E. See Section 3. entry no. 930.

4.A.1185.   Clay, Marie M. See Section 2.C.45. entry no. 642.

4.A.1186.   Clay, Marie M., ed. See Section 2.C.45. entry no. 643.

4.A.1187.   Collins, Cathy, et al. See Section 2.A. entry no. 7.

4.A.1188.   Downing, John. "Children's Concepts of Language in
             Learning to Read." **Educational Research** 12(February
             1970): 106-112.

4.A.1189.   Downing, John. "The Child's Concepts of Language." In
             The Road to Effective Reading. Edited by W. Latham.
             London: Ward Lock Educational, 1974.

4.A.1190.   Durkin, Dolores. "Children Who Read Before Grade I: A
             Second Study." **Elementary School Journal** 64(December
             1963): 143-148.

4.A.1191.   Durkin, Dolores. "A Fifth-Year Report on the Achievement
             of Early Readers." **Elementary School Journal** 65
             (November 1964): 76-80.

4.A.1192.   Durkin, Dolores. "When Should Children Begin to Read?"
             In **Innovation and Change in Reading Instruction,** 67th
             Yearbook of the NSSE, Part 2, pp. 30-71. Edited by
             Helen M. Robinson. Chicago: University of Chicago,
             1968.

4.A.1193.   Gardener, R. C. "Attitudes and Motivation: Their Role in
             Second Language Acquisition." **TESOL Quarterly** 2
             (September 1968): 141-150.

4.A.1194.   Gates, Arthur I. "The Necessary Mental Age for Beginning
             Reading." **Elementary School Journal** 37(March 1937):

497–508.

4.A.1195.   Gates, Arthur I., and Bond, Guy. "Reading Readiness: A
             Study of Factors Determining Success and Failure in
             Beginning Reading." Teachers College Record 37(May
             1936): 679–685.

4.A.1196.   Gattegno, Caleb. Reading with Words in Colour: A
             Scientific Study of the Problems of Reading. Reading:
             Educational Explorers, 1969.

4.A.1197.   Gibson, Eleanor J. "Experimental Psychology of Learning
             to Read." In The Disabled Child: Education of the
             Dyslexic Child. Edited by John Money. Baltimore,
             Maryland: Johns Hopkins Press, 1966.

4.A.1198.   Gillooly, W. B. "The Influence of Writing-System
             Characteristics on Learning to Read." Reading
             Research Quarterly 8(1973): 167–199.

4.A.1199.   Good, T. L., and Brophy, J. E. Do Boys and Girls Receive
             Equal Opportunity in First-Grade Reading Instruction?
             Report Series No. 24. Austin, Texas: Research and
             Development Center for Teacher Education, University
             of Texas, 1969.

4.A.1200.   Johnson, R. D.; Ollila, L. O.; and Downing, J. "The
             Effect of Auditory Discrimination Training on Reading
             Readiness Measures." In Examining and Meeting Today's
             Reading Needs in B.C. Vancouver, B.C.: University of
             British Columbia, 1973.

4.A.1201.   Kerfoot, James F., ed. First Grade Reading Programs.
             Newark, Delaware: International Reading Association,
             1967.

4.A.1202.   King, Ethel M. "Beginning Reading: When and How." The
             Reading Teacher 22(March 1969): 550–553.

4.A.1203.   Kuennaps, Teodor, and Janson, Anne-Jeanette. "Multi-
             dimensional Similarity of Letters." Perceptual Motor
             Skills 28, 1(February 1969): 3–12.

4.A.1204.   Malicky, Grace, and Norman, Charles. "Reading Processes of
             "Natural" Readers." Reading-Canada-Lecture 3, 1(Spring
             1985): 8–20.

4.A.1205.   Manis, F. R., et al. "A Comparison of Analogy and Rule
             Based Decoding Strategies in Normal and Dyslexic
             Children." Journal of Reading Behavior 18, 3(1986):
             203–218.

4.A.1206.   Maxwell, Madeline M. "Beginning Reading and Deaf
             Children." American Annals of the Deaf 131, 1(March
             1986): 14–20.

4.A.1207. Mazurkiewicz, A. J. "Sociocultural Influences and
           Reading." Journal of Developmental Reading 3(1960):
           254-263.

4.A.1208. Miller, G. A. "Free Recall of Redundant Strings of
           Letters." Journal of Experimental Psychology
           56(1958): 484-491.

4.A.1209. Morphett, M. V., and Washburne C. "When Should Children
           Begin to Read?" Elementary School Journal 31(March
           1931): 496-503.

4.A.1210. Nachshon, Israel, et al. "Directional Scanning as a
           Function of Stimulus Characteristics, Reading Habits,
           and Directional Set." Journal of Cross-Cultural
           Psychology 8, 1(March 1977): 83-99.

4.A.1211. Noel, E., ed. Able to Enjoy: Books and the Young.
           Sydney: IBBY Australia, 1982.

4.A.1212. Ollila, Lloyd O. See Section 2.A. entry no. 75.

4.A.1213. Piaget, Jean. "Development of Mental Imagery." In Piaget
           Rediscovered. Edited by R. Ripple and V. Rockcastle.
           Ithaca, New York: Cornell University, 1964.

4.A.1214. Quorn, Kerry Charles, et al. See Section 3 entry no. 1097.

4.A.1215. Rathbone, M. "Parent Participation in the Primary
           School." Educational Studies 7, 2(1981): 145-150.

4.A.1216. Salisbury, D. F., et al. See Section 2.C.26. entry no. 481.

4.A.1217. Seitz, Victoria. Social Class and Ethnic Group
           Differences in Learning to Read. Newark, Delaware:
           International Reading Association, 1977.

4.A.1218. Shvatchkin, N. Kh. "The Development of Phonematic
           Perception of Speech in Young Children." News of the
           Academy of Psychological Science of the Russian Soviet
           Federative Socialist Republic 13(1948).

4.A.1219. Simons, Herbert D. "Black Dialect and Learning to Read."
           In Literacy for Diverse Learners, pp. 3-13. Edited
           by Jerry L. Johns. Newark, Delaware: International
           Reading Association, 1974.

4.A.1220. Smith, Donald E. Learning to Read and Write: A Task
           Analysis. New York: Academic Press, 1976.

4.A.1221. Southgate, Vera, et al. Extending Beginning Reading.
           London: Heinemann Educational Books Ltd., 1981.

4.A.1222. Spache, George D., and Spache, Evelyn B. Reading in the
           Elementary School. Boston, Allyn, 1969.

4.A.1223.   The Teaching of Reading. 12th International Conference on
            Public Education, convened by UNESCO and the Inter-
            national Bureau of Education. Geneva: International
            Bureau of Education, 1949.

4.A.1224.   Wittick, Mildred Letton. "Innovations in Reading
            Instruction: For Beginners." In Innovation and
            Change in Reading Instruction, 67th Yearbook of the
            NSSE, Part 2, pp. 72-125. Edited by Helen M.
            Robinson. Chicago: University of Chicago, 1968.

4.A.1225.   Wynn, Sammye J. "A Beginning Reading Program for the
            Deprived Child." The Reading Teacher 21(October
            1967): 40-47.

4.A.1226.   Young, Beverly S. "A Study of Visual Efficiency Necessary
            for Beginning Reading." Paper presented at the Annual
            Meeting of the Southwest Regional Conference of the
            International Reading Association. San Antonio, Texas:
            1986. ED 268 498.

4.A.1227.   Zelan, Karen. "Thoughts on What Children Bring to
            Reading." Prospects 15, 1(1985): 49-56.

B. TEACHING OF READING

4.B.1228.   Abiri, J. O. O. See Section 2.C.46. entry no. 651.

4.B.1229.   Adams, Mary Lourita. See Section 2.C.69. entry no. 775.

4.B.1230.   Atkinson, R. C. "Teaching Children to Read Using a
            Computer." American Psychologist 29(1974): 3.

4.B.1231.   Barney, W. D. See Section 2.C.45. entry no. 639.

4.B.1232.   Barnitz, John. G. See Section 3. entry no. 909.

4.B.1233.   Bear, David Eli. See Section 3. entry no. 910.

4.B.1234.   Bereiter, Carl, and Englemann, Siegfried. Teaching Dis-
            advantaged Children in the Preschool. Englewood
            Cliffs, New Jersey: Prentice-Hall, 1966.

4.B.1235.   Brogan, Peggy, et al. See Section 4.A. entry no. 1179.

4.B.1236.   Bush, Clifford L., and Huebner, Mildred H. Strategies for
            Reading in the Elementary School. New York:
            Macmillan, 1970.

4.B.1237.   Ceprano, Maria A. "A Review of Selected Research on
            Methods of Teaching Sight Words." The Reading Teacher
            35, 3(December 1981): 314-322.

4.B.1238.   Clapp, R. C. "The Relationship of Teacher Sex to Fifth-
            Grade Boys' Achievement Gains and Attitudes Toward

School." Doctoral dissertation, Stanford University, 1967.

4.B.1239.   Cohen, S. Alan. Teach Them All to Read: Theory, Methods, and Materials for Teaching the Disadvantaged. New York: Random, 1969.

4.B.1240.   Dawson, Mildred. "How Effective is I.T.A. in Reading Instruction?" International Reading Association Conference Proceedings Part 2, 13(April 1968): 224-237.

4.B.1241.   Destefano, Johanna S., et al. Transition into Literacy: An Analysis of Language Behavior During Reading and Writing Instruction in a First Grade Classroom. Paper presented at the Annual Meeting of the International Reading Association. St. Louis: n.p., 1980. ED 186 865.

4.B.1242.   Durkin, Dolores. Teaching Them to Read. Boston: Allyn, 1970.

4.B.1243.   Gagg, J. C., and Gagg, M. E. Teaching Children to Read. London: Newnes, 1955.

4.B.1244.   Gray, W. S. Teaching of Reading and Writing. Chicago: Scott, Foresman, 1956.

4.B.1245.   Hildreth, Gertrude. "Lessons in Arabic." The Reading Teacher 19(December 1965): 202-210.

4.B.1246.   Huey, E. B. The Psychology and Pedagogy of Reading. New York: Macmillan, 1908. Reprinted at Cambridge, Massachusetts: MIT Press, 1968.

4.B.1247.   International Bureau of Education. The Teaching of Reading. Paris: UNESCO, 1949.

4.B.1248.   Jansen, Mogens. See Section 2.C.14. entry no. 259.

4.B.1249.   Kritzer, Richard. See Section 2.A. entry no. 59.

4.B,1250.   Larrick, Nancy. "Children's Literature and the Teaching of Reading." In Reading: Current Research and Practice V-I. Edinburgh: United Kingdom Reading Association, William Blackwood & Sons, 1967.

4.B.1251.   Mathews, Milford M. Teaching to Read: Historically Considered. Chicago: University of Chicago, 1966.

4.B.1252.   Olshtain, Elite. "Teaching Reading in a Foreign Language." In Mother Tongue or Second Language. Edited by Dina Feitelson. Newark, Delaware: International Reading Association, 1979.

4.B.1253.   Reading Conference, 22nd, Lehigh University, 1973. Teach-
             ing Reading: The Growing Diversity. Edited by Joseph
             P. Kender. Danville, Illinois: Interstate Printers
             and Publishers, 1974.

4.B.1254.   Reeves, Noelene, and Bessell-Brown, Thelma, eds. How to
             Teach Reading...And the Year of the Child. Adelaide:
             Australian Reading Association, 1980.

4.B.1255.   Schonell, F. J. The Psychology and Teaching of Reading.
             London: Oliver and Boyd, 1946.

4.B.1256.   Skjelfjord, V. J. See Section 2.C.48. entry no. 671.

4.B.1257.   Smith, Richard J., and Otto, Wayne. "Elementary Teachers'
             Preferences for Pre-Service and In-Service Training
             in the Teaching of Reading." Journal of Educational
             Research 63(July-August 1970): 445-449.

4.B.1258.   Spache, George D. "Contributions of Allied Fields to the
             Teaching of Reading." In Innovations and Change in
             Reading Instruction, pp. 237-290. 67th Yearbook of
             the NSSE, Part 2. Edited by Helen M. Robinson.
             Chicago: University of Chicago, 1968.

4.B.1259.   Strang, Ruth. Diagnostic Teaching of Reading. New York:
             McGraw-Hill, 1969.

4.B.1260.   Taba, Hilda. Teaching Strategies and Cognitive
             Functioning in Elementary School Children.
             Cooperative Research USOE Project No. 2404. San
             Francisco, California: San Francisco State College,
             1966.

4.B.1261.   Tinker, Miles A., and McCullough, Constance M. Teaching
             Elementary Reading, 3rd Edition. New York:
             Appleston, 1968.

4.B.1262.   Ukrskov, M. Gennemgang Af To Loesebogssystemer for
             Danskundervisningen I 3., 4, 5, Og 7. Skolear Ud Fra
             Nogle Indholdsmoessige Og Formelle Kriterier (A Review
             of Two Systems of Reading for the Teaching of Danish
             to Grades 3, 4, 5, and 7 Based on Certain Criteria as
             to Content and Form). Copenhagen: Danmarks
             Poedagogiske Institut (The Danish Institute for Edu-
             cational Research), 1969.

C. MATERIALS

4.C.1263.   Aaron, Robert L., and Anderson, Martha K. "A Comparison
             of Values Expressed in Juvenile Magazines and Basal
             Reader Series." The Reading Teacher 35, 3(December
             1981): 305-313.

4.C.1264. Altwerger, Bess, and Kenneth S. Goodman. Studying Text Difficulty Through Miscue Analysis. Program in Language and Literacy. Occasional Paper Number 3. Tucson, Arizona: Arizona University, College of Education, 1981. ED 209 657.

4.C.1265. Blom, Gaston E., and Wiberg, J. Lawrence. "Attitude Content in Reading Primers." In Comparative Reading, pp. 85-104. Edited by John Downing. New York: Macmillan, 1973.

4.C.1266. Chacko, Chinna. See Section 2.C.43. entry no. 634.

4.C.1267. Coppell B. See Section 2.C.3. entry no. 155.

4.C.1268. Coppell, W. G. See Section 2.C.3. entry no. 156.

4.C.1269. Cox, Juanita, et al. See Section 2.C.69. entry no. 796.

4.C.1270. Eyster, Ira, et al. Culture Through Concepts--A Teachers Guide. Norman, Oklahoma: Oklahoma University, Southwest Center for Human Relations Studies, 1980. ED 176 928.

4.C.1271. Fitzgerald, M. J. "Fairy Tales and Folk Stories: The Significance of Multicultural Elements in Children's Literature." Reading 12, 3(December 1978): 10-21.

4.C.1272. Glaser, Robert. "Instructional Technology and the Measurement of Learning Outcomes: Some Questions." American Psychologist 18(1963): 519-521.

4.C.1273. Hunt, Lyman C., Jr., ed. The Individualized Reading Program. Proceedings of the Annual Convention, No. 11, Vol. 2, Part 3. Newark, Delaware: International Reading Association, 1967.

4.C.1274. January, G. R. See Section 2.C.3. entry no. 169.

4.C.1275. Kogan, Nathan and Chadrow, Mindy. "Children's Comprehension of Metaphor in the Pictoral and Verbal Modality." International Journal of Behavioral Development 9, 3(September 1986): 285-295.

4.C.1276. Lewis, Charles Stephen. The Treatment of Foreign Peoples and Cultures in American High School Literature Books. Ann Arbor, Michigan: University Microfilms, 1957. AC-1, #21,328.

4.C.1277. Lorimer, Rowland. "Publishing and the Canadian Content of Readers." Orbit 10, 4(October 1979): 24-26.

4.C.1278. Lorimer, R., et al. "Consider Content: An Analysis of Two Canadian Primary Language Arts Reading Series." Interchange 8, 4(77-78): 64-77.

4.C.1279.   Manuals for Primary Education.   Geneva: International
             Bureau of Education, 1959.

4.C.1280.   Mehrotra, Preet Vanti.   See Section 2.C.30. entry no. 503.

4.C.1281.   Olson, Willard C.   "Seeking Self-Selection and Pacing in
             the Use of Books by Children."   The Packet 7(Spring
             1952):   3-10.

4.C.1282.   Rusted, Jennifer, and Hodgson, Sandra.   "Evaluating the
             Picture Facilitation Effect in Children's Recall of
             Written Texts."   British Journal of Educational
             Psychology 55, 3(November 1985):   288-294.

4.C.1283.   Ross, R. R.   Reading Disability and Crime: Link and Re-
             mediation: An Annotated Bibliography.   Ottawa:
             Department of Criminology, University of Ottawa, 1977.

4.C.1284.   Sheridan, E. Marcia.   Sex Differences and Readability: An
             Annotated Bibliography.   Newark, Delaware: Inter-
             national Reading Association, 1976.

4.C.1285.   Shiach, G. M.   "Effectiveness of SRA Reading Laboratory
             2a with Boys of Below Average Ability."   Educational
             Research 13, (June 1971):   222-225.

4.C.1286.   Shrodes, Caroline.   "Bibliography."   The Reading Teacher
             9(1955):   24-29.

4.C.1287.   Taiwo, Oladele.   See Section 2.A. entry no. 95.

4.C.1288.   "The Teacher and His Materials: A View of Accountability
             from the Inside."   Elementary School Journal 73, 7
             (April 1973):   347-353.

4.C.1289.   Veatch, Jeanette.   Reading in the Elementary School.   New
             York: Ronald, 1966.

4.C.1290.   Zelan, Karen.   "Hidden and Trick Themes: Children's
             Primers."   Prospects 16, 1(1986):   95-112.

D.   METHOD

4.D.1291.   Artley, A. Sterl.   "Are There Any Real Differences Between
             Reading Instruction in the Elementary School and in
             the High School?"   International Reading Association
             Conference Proceedings Part 2, 13(April 1968):   419-
             430.

4.D.1292.   Austin, Lettie J.   "Reading and Writing for Black Youth."
             Reading Improvement 9, 1(Spring 1972):   45-47.

4.D.1293.   Bamman, Henry A.; Hogan, Ursula; and Greene, Charles B.
             Reading Instruction in the Secondary Schools.   New
             York: McKay, 1961.

4.D.1294.   Barbe, Walter B.   Educator's Guide to Personalized Reading
             Instruction.   Englewood Cliffs, New Jersey: Prentice-
             Hall, 1961.

4.D.1295.   Behrstock, Julian.   "Reaching the Rural Reader."   Journal
             of Reading 24, 8(May 1981):   712-718.

4.D.1296.   "'Buyer Be Wary' Cautions IRA."   The Reading Teacher 20
             (April 1967):   599.

4.D.1297.   Catterson, Jane Hunter.   Inductive Versus Deductive
             Methods in Word Recognition Analysis in Grade Five.
             Ann Arbor, Michigan: University Microfilms, 1959.
             AC-1, 59-6117.

4.D.1298.   Darrow, Helen Fisher, and Howes, Virgil M.   Approaches to
             Individualized Reading.   New York: Appleton, 1960.

4.D.1299.   Davis, O. L., and Slobodian, J. J.   "Teacher Behaviour
             Towards Boys and Girls During First Grade Reading
             Instruction."   American Educational Research Journal
             4(1967):   261-269.

4.D.1300.   Dechant, Emerald V.   Improving the Teaching of Reading.
             2nd Edition.   Englewood Cliffs, New Jersey: Prentice-
             Hall, 1970.

4.D.1301.   Dodds, William J.   "Highlights from the History of Reading
             Instruction."   The Reading Teacher 21(December 1967):
             274-280.

4.D.1302.   Dollerup, C.   "Effects of Prereading Instructions on
             Readers' Responses."   Journal of Reading 23, (November
             1979):   112-120.

4.D.1303.   Elgart, Denise B.   See Section 3. entry no. 962.

4.D.1304.   ERIC Clearinghouse and Retrieval of Information and
             Evaluation on Reading.   Evidence of Effectiveness of
             Existing Practices for Teaching Reading.   Bloomington,
             Indiana: ERIC, 1970.

4.D.1305.   Fausek, U. I.   Learning Literacy and the Development of
             Speech by the Montessori System.   Moscow: Gosizdat,
             1922.

4.D.1306.   Gamez, Gloria I.   "Reading in a Second Language: Native
             Language Approach vs. Direct Method."   The Reading
             Teacher 32, 6(March 1979):   665-670.

4.D.1307.   Goldbecker, Sheralyn S.   Reading: Instructional
             Approaches.   Washington, D.C.:   National Education
             Association, 1975.

4.D.1308.   Graham, Steve.   See Section 3. entry no. 981.

4.D.1309.   Gray, William S. "The Evolution of Patterns of Instruc-
             tional Organization." In Reading Instruction in
             Various Patterns of Grouping, Supplementary
             Educational Monographs, No. 89, pp. 14-19. Edited
             by Helen M. Robinson. Chicago: University of
             Chicago, 1959.

4.D.1310.   Guszak, Frank J. "Teachers' Questions and Levels of Read-
             ing Comprehension." In The Measurement of Children's
             Achievement, Perspectives in Reading, No. 8, pp. 97-
             109. Newark, Delaware: International Reading
             Association, 1967.

4.D.1311.   Harris, A. J., and Morrison, C. "The CRAFT Project: A
             Final Report." The Reading Teacher 22(February 1969):
             335-340.

4.D.1312.   Huus, Helen. "Innovations in Reading Instruction: At
             Later Levels." In Innovation and Change in Reading
             Instruction, 67th Yearbook of the NSSE, Part 2, pp.
             126-158. Edited by Helen M. Robinson. Chicago:
             University of Chicago, 1968.

4.D.1313.   Lewis, Edward R. Initial Teaching Alphabet (I.T.A.) for
             Instruction of Reading Disability Cases. San Jose,
             California: San Jose State College, 1964. ED 003
             854.

4.D.1314.   Livingston, Howard. "An Investigation of the Effect of
             Instruction in General Semantics on Critical Reading
             Ability." California Journal of Educational Research
             16(March 1965): 93-96.

4.D.1315.   Lloyd, Helene M. "Reading Instruction for the
             Disadvantaged: Is It Adequate?" In Current Issues in
             Reading, pp. 134-147. Edited by Nila B. Smith.
             Newark, Delaware: International Reading Association,
             1969.

4.D.1316.   Mazurkiewicz, Albert J. First Grade Reading Using
             Modified Co-Basal Versus the Initial Teaching
             Alphabet. Bethlehem, Pennsylvania: Lehigh
             University, 1965.

4.D.1317.   McCullough, Constance M. "What Does Research in Reading
             Reveal About Practices in Teaching Reading?" English
             Journal 58(May 1969): 688-706.

4.D.1318.   Muller, H. Methoden Des Erstleseunterrichts Und Ihre
             Ergebnisse. Munich: Ernest Reinhardt Verlag, 1961.

4.D.1319.   Parsons, James, and Tomas, Douglas. "Reading in the
             Social Studies: What Not to Do." History and Social
             Science Teacher 13, 3(Spring 1978): 175-179.

4.D.1320.   Peters, Margaret. "The Influence of Reading Methods on
             Spelling." British Journal of Educational Psychology
             37(February 1967): 47–53.

4.D.1321.   Pumfrey, Peter David. Reading: Tests and Assessment
             Techniques. London: Hodder and Stoughton for the
             United Kingdom Reading Association, 1976.

4.D.1322.   Rawl, Ruth K., and O'Tuel, Frances S. "A Comparison of
             Three Prereading Approaches for Kindergarten Students."
             Reading Improvement 19, 3(Fall 1982): 205–211.

4.D.1323.   Reid, J., ed. Reading: Problems and Practices. London:
             Ward Lock, 1972.

4.D.1324.   Robinson, Helen M., ed. Reading Instruction in Various
             Patterns of Grouping, Supplementary Educational
             Monographs, No. 89. Chicago: University of Chicago,
             1959.

4.D.1325.   Saadeh, Ibraham Q. "The Teacher and the Development of
             Critical Thinking." Journal of Research and Develop-
             ment in Education 3(Fall 1969): 87–99.

4.D.1326.   Sartain, Harry W. "Organizational Patterns of Schools and
             Classrooms for Reading Instruction." In Innovation
             and Change in Reading Instruction, pp. 195–236. 67th
             Yearbook of the NSSE, Part 2. Edited by Helen M.
             Robinson. Chicago: University of Chicago, 1968.

4.D.1327.   Shane, Harold G. "Grouping in the Elementary School."
             Phi Delta Kappan 41(April 1960): 313–318.

4.D.1328.   Southgate, V. "Approaching I.T.A. Results with Caution."
             Educational Research 7(1965): 83–96.

4.D.1329.   Staiger, Ralph C. "The Geology of Reading." In The
             Second International Reading Symposium. Edited by
             John Downing and Amy L. Brown. London: Cassell,
             1967.

4.D.1330.   Stauffer, Russell G., ed. Individualized Reading Instruc-
             tion. Proceedings of the 39th Annual Conference,
             Vol. 6. Newark, Delaware: Reading–Study Center,
             University of Delaware, 1957.

4.D.1331.   Strang, Ruth. "How Successful Readers Learn." In Read-
             ing: A Human Right and a Human Problem, pp. 15–20.
             Edited by Ralph C. Staiger and Oliver Andresen.
             Newark, Delaware: International Reading Association,
             1969.

4.D.1332.   Veatch, Jeanette. Individualizing Your Reading Program.
             New York: Putnam, 1959.

4.D.1333.   Walshe, R. D., ed. **The New English: How to...** Sydney,
            Australia: Primary English Teaching Association of
            N.S.W., 1976.

4.D.1334.   Yates, Alfred, ed. **Grouping in Education.** New York:
            Wiley, 1966.

E. BASAL

4.E.1335.   Abiri, J. O. O. See Section 2.C.46. entry no. 651.

4.E.1336.   Durkin, Dolores. "Reading Comprehension Instruction in
            Five Basal Reader Series." **Reading Research Quarterly**
            16, 4(1981): 515-544.

4.E.1337.   Fillmer, H. Thompson, and Meadaus, Rita. "The Portrayal of
            Older Characters in Five Sets of Basal Readers."
            Elementary School Journal 86, 5(May 1986): 651-662.

4.E.1338.   Fry, Edward Bernard. See Section 3 entry no. 973.

4.E.1339.   Hall, Nigel. "Characters in British Basal Series Don't
            Read Either." **The Reading Teacher** 37, (October 1983):
            22-25.

4.E.1340.   Hynd, Cynthia R., and Carter, Sylvia M. "Content Analysis
            of Two Reading Series for Disabled Readers." **Reading
            World** 23, 1(October 1983): 29-35.

4.E.1341.   Mazurkiewicz, Albert J. See Section 4.D. entry no. 1316.

4.E.1342.   McPherson, Jane A. "Questioning Techniques and Teaching
            Strategies Using the Ginn Basal Reading Series--
            Comparative Study in Canadian and British Elementary/
            Primary Schools." Vancouver: Educational Research
            Institute of British Columbia, 1981.

4.E.1343.   Rogers, Arnold R. See Section 3. entry no. 1106.

4.E.1344.   Sabaroff, Rose. E. See Section 3. entry no. 1110.

4.E.1345.   Schwartz, R., et al. See Section 2.C.23. entry no. 470.

4.E.1346.   Sheldon, William D. See Section 3. entry no. 1119.

4.E.1347.   Spencer Doris U., et al. See Section 3. entry no. 1126.

4.E.1348.   Stauffer, Russell G., et al. See Section 3. entry no.
            1130.

4.E.1349.   Warren, Ann, et al. See Section 3. entry no. 1156.

4.E.1350.   Wyatt, Nita M. See Section 3, entry no. 1165.

F. INDIVIDUALIZED READING

4.F.1351.   Spencer, Doris U., et al. See Section 3 entry no. 1126.

4.F.1352.   Stauffer, Russell G., ed. See Section 4.D. entry no. 1320.

4.F.1353.   Veatch, Jeanette. See Section 4.D. entry no. 1332.

4.F.1354.   Warren, Ann, et al. See Section 3. entry no. 1156.

G. I.T.A.

4.G.1355.   Chasnoff, Robert E. See Section 3. entry no. 930.

4.G.1356.   Dawson, Mildred. See Section 4.B. entry no. 1240.

4.G.1357.   Downing, J. "New Alphabet Helps Beginning Readers; Initial
             Teaching Alphabet." The Catholic School Journal 63,
             (September 1963): 46–48.

4.G.1358.   Downing, John. See Section 2.C.17. entry no. 302.

4.G.1359.   Ellis, E. N. See Section 3. entry no. 964.

4.G.1360.   "I.T.A. Crusader Returns to do Battle." Times Educational
             Supplement, 2779: 319, August 23, 1968.

4.G.1361.   Robertson, Douglas J., and Trepper, Terry Steven. "The
             Effects of I.T.A. on the Reading Achievement of
             Mexican–American Children." Reading World 14, 2
             (December 1974): 132–138.

4.G.1362.   Trepper, Terry Steven, et al. See Section 7.H. entry
             no. 1617.

H. L.E.A.

4.H.1363.   Edwards, Thomas J. "Language-Experience Attack on
             Cultural Deprivation." In Remedial Reading: An
             Anthology of Sources, pp. 279–285. Edited by Leo M.
             Shell and Paul C. Burns. Boston: Allyn, 1968.

4.H.1364.   Garcia, Ricardo L. See Section 7.H. entry no. 1612.

4.H.1365.   Haynes, C. S. See Section 10.D. entry no. 1757.

4.H.1366.   Marita, Sister. See Section 3. entry no. 1053.

4.H.1367.   Pienaar, P. T. See Section 2.C.59. entry no. 714.

I. LINGUISTIC

4.I.1368.   Sabaroff, Rose. E. See Section 3. entry no. 1110.

4.I.1369.   Seymour, Dorothy Z.   See Section 3. entry no. 1115.

4.I.1370.   Sheldon, William D., et al.   See Section 3. entry no.
             1119.

4.I.1371.   Wyatt, Nita M.   See Section 3. entry no. 1165.

J.   PHONICS

4.J.1372.   Amoroso, Henry C., Jr.   "Phonetically Justified Spelling
             Strategies of Good and Poor Readers in the Third
             Grade." **Research in Rural Education** 3, 2(Winter 1985):
             75-78.

4.J.1373.   Gale, M. A.   See Section 2.C.3. entry no. 165.

4.J.1374.   Kochnower, Jeffrey, et al.   "A Comparison of the Phonic
             Decoding Ability of Normal and Learning Disabled
             Children." **Journal of Learning Disabilities** 16,
             6(June-July 1983):   348-351.

4.J.1375.   Seymour, Dorothy Z.   See Section 3. entry no. 1115.

5

Correlates of Basic Skills

A. BASIC SKILLS

5.A.1376.   Berglund, Gosta W. "On Basic Skills." **Practical Applica-tions of Research** 1(March 1980): 3. (Newsletter of Phi Delta Kappa's Center on Evaluation, Development and Research).

5.A.1377.   Braam, Leonard S., and Roehm, Marilyn A. "Subject-Area Teachers' Familiarity with Reading Skills." **Journal of Developmental Reading** 7(Spring 1964): 188-196.

5.A.1378.   Gibson, E. J.; Osser, H.; and Pick, A. D. "A Study in the Development of Grapheme-Phoneme Correspondence." **Journal of Verbal Learning and Verbal Behaviour** 2 (1963): 142-146.

5.A.1379.   Gibson, Eleanor J.; Pick, Anne; Osser, Harry; and Hammond, Marcia. "The Role of Grapheme-Phoneme Correspondence in the Perception of Words." **American Journal of Psychology** 75(1962): 554-570.

5.A.1380.   Halle, Morris. "Some Thoughts on Spelling." In **Psycho-linguistics and the Teaching of Reading**, p. 18. Edited by Kenneth S. Goodman and James T. Fleming. Newark, Delaware: International Reading Association, 1968.

5.A.1381.   Herber, Harold L., comp. and ed. **Developing Study Skills in Secondary Schools, Perspectives in Reading, No. 4.** Newark, Delaware: International Reading Association, 1965.

5.A.1382.   Hoepfner, Ralph, et al. **The Sample for the Sustaining Effects Study and Projections of Its Characteristics to the National Population. Overview of Technical Report No. 1 from the Study of the Sustaining Effects**

of Compensatory Education and Basic Skills. Santa
Monica, California: Systems Development Corporation,
1977, ED 146 183.

5.A.1383. Hollingsworth, Paul M. "Interrelating Listening and Reading." International Reading Association Conference
Proceedings, Part 1, 13(April 1968): 63-67.

5.A.1384. Kintsch, Walter, and Kozminsky, Ely. "Summarizing Stories
After Reading and Listening." Journal of Educational
Psychology 69, 5(October 1977): 491-499.

5.A.1385. Morioka, Kenji. "Readability and Listenability." In The
Esthetics of Language, pp. 209-248. Edited by Endo
Yoshimoto. Tokyo: Nakayama Shoten, 1958.

5.A.1386. Olson, Arthur V. "School Achievement, Reading Ability,
and Specific Visual Perception Skills in the Third
Grade." The Reading Teacher 19(April 1966): 490-
492.

5.A.1387. Ramsey, Wallace, and Harrod, Dorothy. "Diagnostic
Measures of Phonic Analysis Skills." International
Reading Association Conference Proceedings, Part 1,
13(April 1968): 642-645.

5.A.1388. Ramsey, Z. Wallace. "Will Tomorrow's Teachers Know and
Teach Phonics?" The Reading Teacher 15(January 1962):
241-245.

5.A.1389. Rawal, R. T. The Basic Vocabulary of Gujarati Children
at the Age of 12 Plus. Bombay: University of Bombay,
1959.

5.A.1390. Samuels, S. Jay. "Recognition of Flashed Words by
Children." Child Development 41, 4(December 1970):
89-94.

5.A.1391. Stewart, Bob R., et al. "Influence of Reading Ability and
Verbal Modality on Principle Learning of Vocational
Students." Journal of Industrial Teacher Education
13, 3(Spring 1976): 48-55.

5.A.1392. Wright, Ian. "Capture: A Game using Map Reading Skills."
History and Social Science Teacher 13, 4(Summer 1978):
288-290.

5.A.1393. Zeman, Samuel S. "Reading Comprehension and Writing of
Second and Third Graders." The Reading Teacher 23,
23(November 1969): 144-150.

5.A.1394. Zhuravleva, R. Ia. "The Mastery of Spelling." Soviet
Education 19, (February/March/April 1977): 165-181.

B.   LANGUAGE ARTS

5.B.1395.   Downing, John. See Section 2.C.17. entry no. 305.

5.B.1396.   Grundin, Hans U. "The Development of Reading and Writing
             Abilities in Adutls." In Reading: Research and
             Classroom Practice, pp. 127-137. Edited by John
             Gilliland. (Proceedings of the Thirteenth Annual
             Course and Conference of the United Kingdom Reading
             Association), 1977.

5.B.1397.   Smith, Nila Banton. "Patterns of Writing in Different
             Subject Areas--Part I." Journal of Reading 8(October
             1964): 31-37.

5.B.1398.   Smith, Nila Banton. "Patterns of Writing in Different
             Subject-Areas--Part II." Journal of Reading 8
             November 1964): 97-102.

C.   KANA LETTERS

5.C.1399.   Matsubara, Tatsuya, et al. See Section 2.C.36. entry no.
             579.

5.C.1400.   Matsubara, Tatsuya, et al. See Section 2.C.36. entry no.
             580.

5.C.1401.   Sakamoto, Takhiko, et al. See Section 2.C.36. entry no.
             611.

D.   KATAKANA LETTERS

5.D.1402.   Sakamoto, Takahiko, et al. See Section 2.C.36. entry no.
             612.

E.   TRADITIONAL COMMUNICATION SYMBOLS

5.E.1403.   Chasnoff, Robert E. See Section 3. entry no. 930.

5.E.1404.   Hildreth, Gertrude. See Section 2.C.62. entry no. 728.

5.E.1405.   Kuromaru, S., et al. See Section 2.C.36. entry no. 577.

5.E.1406.   Matsubara, Tatsuya, et al. See Section 2.C.36. entry no.
             579.

5.E.1407.   Matsubara, Tatsuya, et al. See Section 2.C.36. entry no.
             580.

5.E.1408.   Muraishi, Shozo, et al. See Section 2.C.36. entry no.
             582.

5.E.1409.   Muraishi, Shozo, et al. See Section 2.C.36. entry no. 583.

5.E.1410.   Sheridan, E. Marcia. See Section 2.A. entry no. 88.

F. TRADITIONAL ORTHOGRAPHIES

5.F.1411.   Ellis, E. N. See Section 3. entry no. 964.

5.F.1412.   Kirkland, Eleanor R. See Section 3. entry no. 1030.

5.F.1413.   Makita, Kiyoshi. "Dyslexia and Orthography." In **Reading: What of the Future?**, pp. 243-248. Edited by Donald Moyle. London: United Kingdom Reading Association, 1975.

5.F.1414.   Thackray, Derek V. See Section 3. entry no. 1138.

G. WORD STUDY

5.G.1415.   Aaron, Ira E. See Section 2.C.69. entry no. 772.

5.G.1416.   "The Alphabetic Principle in Hebrew and German Contrasted to the Alphabetic Principle in English. See Section 2.C.23. entry no. 434.

5.G.1417.   Barnitz, John G. See Section 3. entry no. 909.

5.G.1418.   Harris, Albert J., et. al. See Section 3 entry no. 996.

5.G.1419.   Johns, Jerry L. See Section 3. entry no. 1018.

5.G.1420.   Miller, G. A.; Bruner, J. S.; and Postman, L. "Familiarity of Letter Sequences and Tachistoscopic Identification." **Journal of Genetic Psychology** 50 (1954): 129-139.

6

Correlates of Language

A. LANGUAGE ·

6.A.1421. Athey, Irene J. "Language Models and Reading." **Reading Research Quarterly** VII, 1(Fall 1971): 16-110.

6.A.1422. Chao, Y. R. **Language and Symoblic Systems.** London and New York: Cambridge University Press, 1968.

6.A.1423. Critchley, M. "The Evolution of Man's Capacity for Language." In **Evolution of Man, Volume II.** Edited by S. Tax. Chicago: University of Chicago, 1960.

6.A.1424. Crystal, David. "Neglected Linguistic Principles in the Study of Reading." In **Reading: What of the Future?**, pp. 26-34. Edited by Donald Moyle. London: United Kingdom Reading Association, 1975.

6.A.1425. Dewey, G. **Relative Frequency of English Speech Sounds.** Cambridge, Massachusetts: Harvard University Press, 1923.

6.A.1426. Downing, John. "Linguistic Environments, I." In **Comparative Reading**, pp. 181-216. Edited by John Downing. New York: Macmillan, 1973.

6.A.1427. Downing, John. "Linguistics Environments, II." In **Comparative Reading**, pp. 217-243. Edited by John Downing. New York: Macmillan, 1973.

6.A.1428. Downing, John, and Valtin, R., eds. **Language Awareness and Learning to Read.** New York: Springer-Verlag, 1984.

6.A.1429. Feitelson, Dina, ed. **Mother Tongue or Second Language?** Newark, Delaware: International Reading Association, 1979.

6.A.1430.   Findley, Warren G. Language: Friend or Foe? Discussion
            of papers at NCME Symposium on "The International
            Educational Achievement Study; Methodological Issues
            and Selected Results." Chicago: n.p., 1974. Ed 103
            462.

6.A.1431.   Finocchiaro, Mary. English as a Second Language: From
            Theory to Practice. New York: Regents Publishing
            Co., 1964.

6.A.1432.   Goodman, Kenneth S. "Dialect Barriers to Reading Compre-
            hension." In Teaching Black Children to Read, pp.
            14-28. Edited by Joan C. Baratz and Roger W. Shuy.
            Washington, D.C.: Center for Applied Linguistics,
            1969.

6.A.1433.   Maas-de Brouwer, T. A., and Samson-Sluiter, D. M. M. "Some
            Remarks About the Testing of Reading in a Foreign
            Language." Reading 12, 3(December 1978): 31-35.

6.A.1434.   Miller-Jones, Cynthia. "Untangling the Correlational
            Relationship Between Language and Reading Acquisition."
            Remedial and Special Education 5, 3(May-June 1984):
            50-59.

6.A.1435.   Mitchem, Virginia. "Children of the Earth." The Reading
            Teacher 34, 7(April 1981): 756-761.

6.A.1436.   Morris, Joyce. "Barriers to Successful Reading for
            Second-Language Students at the Secondary Level."
            TESOL Quarterly 2(September 1968): 158-162.

6.A.1437.   Nilagupta, Sirirat. "The Relationship of Syntax to Read-
            ability for ESL Students in Thailand." In Cross-
            Cultural Perspectives on Reading and Reading Research,
            pp. 89-102. Edited by Dina Feitelson. Newark,
            Delaware: International Reading Association, 1978.

6.A.1438.   Pack, Alice C., ed. TESL Reporter 6, 4(1973). ED 083
            877.

6.A.1439.   Robinson, Gail L. See Section 2.A. entry no. 83.

6.A.1440.   Rosen, C. L., and Ortego, P. D. "Language and Reading
            Problems of Spanish Speaking Children in the
            Southwest." Journal of Reading Behavior 1(Winter
            1969): 51-70.

6.A.1441.   Srinivasachari, G. "Selection of Words and Structures for
            Readers." In Reading: A Human Right and Human
            Problem, pp. 80-86. Edited by Ralph C. Staiger and
            Oliver Andresen. Newark, Delaware: International
            Reading Association, 1969.

6.A.1442.   Tyler, V. Lynn, and Taylor, James S. **Reading Between the Lines: Language Indicators Project. Interim Research Summary.** Provo, Utah: Eyring Research Institute, 1978. ED 175 254.

6.A.1443.   Vattakavanich, Pornthip, and Tucker, Albert B. "English as a Second Language vs. Bilingual Education." **Reading Improvement** 17, 4(Winter 1980): 292-294.

B. READABILITY

6.B.1444.   Daines, Delva, et al. See Section 3. entry no. 939.

6.B.1445.   Obonai, Torao, et al. See Section 2.C.36. entry no. 586.

6.B.1446.   Yoloye, E. Ayotunde. See Section 2.B.1. entry no. 115.

C. COMPREHENSION

6.C.1447.   Cleland, Donald L. "A Construct of Comprehension." In **Reading and Inquiry,** Proceedings of the Annual Convention. No. 10, pp. 59-64. Edited by J. Allen Figurel. Newark, Delaware: International Reading Association, 1965.

6.C.1448.   Davis, F. B. "Research in Comprehension in Reading." **Reading Research Quarterly** 3(1968): 499-545.

6.C.1449.   Deblock, A. See Section 3. entry no. 942.

6.C.1450.   Fitzgerald, Thomas, et al. See Section 2.A. entry no. 22.

6.C.1451.   Griese, Arnold A. **Special Problems of Reading Comprehension in the Education of Eskimo and Indian Children.** Alaska: Northern Cross Cultural Education Symposium, 1974. ED 094 918.

6.C.1452.   Harris, Larry A., and Niles, Jerome A. "An Analysis of Published Informal Reading Inventories." **Reading Horizons** 22, 3(Spring 1982): 159-174.

6.C.1453.   Liu, Stella S. F. "Decoding and Comprehension in Reading Chinese." In **Cross-Cultural Perspectives on Reading and Reading Research,** pp. 144-156. Edited by Dina Feitelson. Newark, Delaware: International Reading Association, 1978.

6.C.1454.   Simons, H. D. "Reading Comprehension: The Need for a New Perspective." **Reading Research Quarterly** 6(1971): 338-363.

6.C.1455.   Smith, Nila Banton. "The Many Faces of Reading Comprehension." **The Reading Teacher** 23, 3(December 1969): 249-259.

D. VOCABULARY

6.D.1456.   Dale, Edgar, and Razik Taher. **Bibliography of Vocabulary Studies.** 2nd Edition. Columbus, Ohio: Bureau of Educational Research, Ohio State University, 1963.

6.D.1457.   Dinnan, James. See Section 3. entry no. 944.

6.D.1458.   Harris, Albert J., et al. See Section 3. entry no. 996.

6.D.1459.   Karvonen, J. See Section 2.C.20. entry no. 396.

6.D.1460.   Olander, Herbert T., et al. See Section 3. entry no. 1078.

E. BILINGUALISM

6.E.1461.   Charis, Constantine P. "The Problem of Bilingualism in Modern Greek Education." **Comparative Education Review** 20(1976): 216-219.

6.E.1462.   Diaz, Joseph O. See Section 2.C.69. entry no. 799.

6.E.1463.   Goodman, Kenneth S.; Goodman, Yetta; and Flores, Barbara. **Reading in the Bilingual Classroom: Literacy and Biliteracy.** Rosslyn, Virginia: National Clearinghouse for Bilingual Education, 1979.

6.E.1464.   Markowitz, Alan, and Haley, Frances. **A Bilingual Navajo Curriculum Project. Profiles of Promise 16.** Boulder, Colorado: ERIC Clearinghouse for Social Studies/ Social Science Education, Social Science Education Consortium, Inc., 1973. ED 095 073.

6.E.1465.   Mortensen, E. "Reading Achievement of Native Spanish- Speaking Elementary Students in Bilingual vs. Monolingual Programs." **Bilingual Review** 11(September/ December 1984): 31-36.

6.E.1466.   Titone, Renzo. "Early Bilingual Reading." **Prospects** 15, 1(1985): 67-76.

6.E.1467.   Vattakavanich, Pornthip, et al. See Section 6.A. entry no. 1443.

F. FOREIGN LANGUAGE

6.F.1468.   de Brouwer, T. A. Maas, and Stinter, D. M. M. Sainson. "Some Remarks about the Testing of Reading in a Foreign Language." **Reading** 12, 3(December 1978): 31-35.

6.F.1469.   Feitelson, Dina. See Section 6.A. entry no. 1429.

6.F.1470.   Finocchiaro, Mary. **Teaching English as a Second Language.**
            New York: Harper, 1958.

6.F.1471.   Vattakavanich, Pornthip, et al. See Section 6.A. entry
            no. 1443.

G. ARABIC

6.G.1472.   Hildreth, Gertrude. See Section 4.B. entry no. 1245.

H. CHINESE

6.H.1473.   Downey, T. J. See Section 2.C.28. entry no. 485.

6.H.1474.   Ho, Shang H. "Comments on Teaching Chinese Reading."
            Journal of the Chinese Language Teachers Association
            11, 1(February 1976): 52-57.

6.H.1475.   Liu, Stella S. F. See Section 6.C. entry no. 1453.

6.H.1476.   Schwedel, Allan M. See Section 2.C.28. entry no. 496.

6.H.1477.   Tzeng, Ovid J. L., et al. "Reading the Chinese Characters:
            An Information Processing View." **Journal of Chinese
            Linguistics** 6, 2(June 1978): 287-305.

6.H.1478.   Zhigong, Zhang. "Chinese Characters and Reading: An Out-
            line." **Chinese Education** 18, 2(1985): 41-56.

I. DANISH

6.I.1479.   Jansen, M. "Two Essential Problems in Language Teaching."
            **International Reading Association Conference Proceed-
            ings** 13, Part 1, 1969, 856-863.

6.I.1480.   Jansen, M., and Leerskov, A. **Ti Ars Tidskriftartikler Om
            Danskundervisning Bornehaveklasse--7Skolear (The
            Teaching of Danish Mother Tongue, "First Language," as
            It Appears in Ten Years of Educational Journals and
            Periodicals).** Copenhagen: Danish Institute for
            Educational Research, 1970.

J. ENGLISH

6.J.1481.   "Alphabetic Principle in Hebrew and German Contrasted to
            the Alphabetic Principle in English." See Section
            2.C.23. entry no. 434.

6.J.1482.   Downey, T. J. See Section 2.C.28. entry no. 485.

6.J.1483.   Nance, A. D. See Section 2.C.69. entry no. 837.

6.J.1484.   Vattakavanich, Pornthip, et al. See Section 6.A. entry
                no. 1443.

K. FLEMISH

6.K.1485.   Deblock, A., et al. See Section 3. entry no. 942.

L. FRENCH

6.L.1486.   International Association for the Evaluation of Educational
                Achievement. See Section 2.A. entry no. 42.

M. GERMAN

6.M.1487.   "The Alphabetic Principle in Hebrew and German Contrasted
                to the Alphabetic Principle in English." See Section
                2.C.23. entry no. 434.

6.M.1488.   Archer, Julie, et al. See Section 2.C.23. entry no. 435.

6.M.1489.   Ghendea, Voichita. "Relationships Between Mother Tongue
                (Romanian) and Foreign Language (German) in Developing
                Rational Reading Skills in German." **Issues in Applied
                Psycholinguistics** 17, 2-3(September/December 1985):
                125-134.

N. GUJARATI

6.N.1490.   Lakdawala, V. T. See Section 2.C.30. entry no. 501.

6.N.1491.   Lakdawala, V. T. See Section 2.C.30. entry no. 502.

6.N.1492.   Rawal, R. T. See Section 2.C.30. entry no. 506.

6.N.1493.   Vakil, K. S. See Section 2.C.30. entry no. 511.

O. HINDI

6.O.1494.   Mehrotra, Preet Vanti. See Section 2.C.30. entry no. 503.

P. HEBREW

6.P.1495.   "The Alphabetic Principle in Hebrew and German Contrasted
                to the Alphabetic Principle in English." See Section
                2.C.23. entry no. 434.

6.P.1496.   Eshel, Rina. "Effects of Contextual Richness on Word
                Recognition in Pointed and Unpointed Hebrew." **Reading
                Psychology** 6, 3-4(1985): 127-143.

6.P.1497.   Fijalkow, Jacques. "La Complexite des Relations Grapho-
             phonetiques explique-t-elle les difficultes
             d'apprentissage de al lecture? Le cas de l'hebrew en
             Israel. (De Complexity of Grapho-Phonetic
             Correspondence Explain Problems in Early Reading? The
             Case of Hebrew in Israel.) **Journal of Research in
             Reading** 3, 1(February 1980): 52-59.

Q. JAPANESE

6.Q.1498.   Imura, T. "Aphasia, Its Specificity in Japanese
             Language." **Psychiatria et Neurologia Japonica** 47
             (1943): 196-212.

6.Q.1499.   Sakamoto, Takahiko. See Section 2.C.36. entry no. 604.

R. KOREAN

6.R.1500.   Sakamoto, S. See Section 2.C.36. entry no. 603.

6.R.1501.   Tzeng, Ovid J. L., et al. See Section 2.C.36. entry no. 621.

S. PUNJABI

6.S.1502.   Fukuzawa, Shusuke. See Section 2.C.36. entry no. 572.

6.S.1503.   Sakamoto, S. See Section 2.C.36. entry no. 603.

6.S.1504.   Sakamoto, Takahiko. See Section 2.C.36. entry no. 604.

6.S.1505.   Tzeng, Ovid J. L., et al. See Section 2.C.36. entry no.
             621.

T. SPANISH

6.T.1506.   Gilliam, Bettye, et al. "The Fry Graph Applied to Spanish
             Readability." **The Reading Teacher** 33, 4(January
             1980): 426-430.

6.T.1507.   Hester, K. B. See Section 2.C.69. entry no. 812.

6.T.1508.   Mortensen, E. See Section 6.E. entry no. 1465.

6.T.1509.   Ramirez, Arnulto, G. "Teaching Reading in Spanish: A
             Study of Teacher Effectiveness." **Reading Improvement**
             16, 4(Winter 1979): 304-313.

6.T.1510.   Schon, Isabel. "Science Trade Books in Spanish: An
             Update." **Science and Children** 23, 6(March 1986): 31-
             32.

6.T.1511.   Schon, Isabel, et al. "The Effects of Spanish Reading
            Emphasis on the English and Spanish Reading Abilities
            of Hispanic High School Students." **Bilingual Review**
            11, 1(January-April 1984): 33-39.

6.T.1512.   Wooden, S. L., et al. See Section 12.B. entry no. 1947.

U. HIGHER LEVEL READING SKILLS

6.U.1513.   Burton, W. H.; Kimball, R. B.; and Wing, R. L. Education
            for Effective Thinking. New York: Appleton, 1960.

6.U.1514.   Chase, Francis S. "Demands on the Reader in the Next
            Decade." In Controversial Issues in Reading and
            Promising Solutions, Supplementary Educational Mono-
            graphs, No. 91, pp. 7-18. Edited by Helen M.
            Robinson. Chicago: University of Chicago, 1961.

6.U.1515.   Flanders, Ned. "Teacher Influence in the Classroom." In
            Interaction Analysis: Theory, Research and
            Application. Edited by Edmund J. Amidon and John
            Hough. Reading, Massachusetts: Addison-Wesley, 1967.

6.U.1516.   Glaser, E. M. An Experiment in the Development of
            Critical Thinking, Contributions to Education, No.
            843. New York: Bureau of Publications, Teachers
            College, Columbia University, 1941.

6.U.1517.   Guthrie, John T. "Research: Learning to Criticize
            Literature." Journal of Reading 24, 1(October 1980):
            92-94.

6.U.1518.   Harvison, Alan R. "Critical Reading for Elementary
            Pupils. " The Reading Teacher 21(December 1967):
            244-247.

6.U.1519.   Huelsman, Charles B., Jr. "Promoting Growth in Ability to
            Interpret When Reading Critically: In Grades Seven to
            Ten." In Promoting Growth Toward Maturity in Inter-
            preting What Is Read, Supplementary Educational
            Monographs, No. 74, pp. 149-153. Edited by William
            S. Gray. Chicago: University of Chicago, 1951.

6.U.1520.   Lorge, Irving. "The Teacher's Task in the Development of
            Thinking." The Reading Teacher 13(February 1960):
            170-175.

6.U.1521.   Mueller, Ruth G. "Personality Attributes and Teacher
            Training as They Relate to Pupil Cognitive Skill
            Development of Critical Reading Ability." Ph.D.
            Dissertation, Cleveland, Ohio. Case Western Reserve
            University, 1970.

6.U.1522.   Robinson, Helen M. "Developing Critical Readers." In
            Dimensions of Critical Reading, pp. 1-12. Edited by

Russell Stauffer. Newark, Delaware: University of
Delaware, 1964.

6.U.1523.   Russell, David H. **Children's Thinking.** Boston: Ginn,
1956.

6.U.1524.   Russell, David H. "The Prerequisite: Knowing How to Read
Critically." **Elementary English** 40(October 1963):
579–582.

6.U.1525.   Saadeh, Ibraham Q. See Section 4.D. entry no. 1325.

6.U.1526.   Sanders, Norris M. **Classroom Questions.** New York:
Harper, 1966.

6.U.1527.   Schreiber, Joan E. "Teachers' Question-Asking Techniques
in Social Studies." **Dissertation Abstracts,** No. 28:
523–A. Iowa City, Iowa: University of Iowa, 1967.

6.U.1528.   Wolf, Willavene. "The Logical Dimension of Critical Read-
ing." In **Reading and Inquiry,** Proceedings of the
Annual Convention, No. 10, pp. 121–124. Edited by J.
Allen Figurel. Newark, Delaware: International
Reading Association, 1965.

6.U.1529.   Wolf, Willavene. "A Factor Analytic Study of the Ohio
State University Critical Reading Tests." **Journal of
Research and Development in Education** 3(Fall 1969):
100–109.

6.U.1530.   Wolf, Willavene, et al. See Section 2.C.69. entry no. 879.

7

Correlates of Culture

A. CULTURAL CORRELATES

7.A.1531.   Adiel, S. See Section 2.C.33. entry no. 539.

7.A.1532.   Ayodele, Samuel O. "Reading Characteristics of Learners
            from Two Widely Differing Backgrounds." Reading 18,
            2(July 1984): 115-127.

7.A.1533.   Blanchard P. "Reading Disabilities in Relation to Mal-
            adjustment." Mental Hygiene 12(1928): 772-788.

7.A.1534.   Bledsoe, Joseph. "An Investigation of Six Correlates of
            Student Withdrawl from High School." Journal of
            Educational Research 53(September 1959): 3-6.

7.A.1535.   Bloom, Benjamin S. Stability and Change in Human
            Characteristics. New York: Wiley, 1964.

7.A.1536.   D'Andrade, R. "Sex Differences and Cultural
            Institutions." In The Development of Sex Differences.
            Edited by E. Maccoby. Stanford, California: Stanford
            University Press, 1966.

7.A.1537.   Deckert, Glenn D. See Section 2.C.31. entry no. 512.

7.A.1538.   Deutsch, Martin. "The Role of Social Class in Language
            Development and Cognition." American Journal of
            Orthopsychiatry 35(January 1965): 78-88.

7.A.1539.   Eaves, June. "Reading Disability and Social Adjustment in
            Intelligent Children." Educational Studies 4, 1
            (March 1978): 45-51.

7.A.1540.   Eisenberg, L. "Reading Retardation: I. Psychiatric and
            Sociologic Aspects." Pediatrics 37(1966): 352-365.

7.A.1541.   Ellison, Tom, and Wilson, Gerald. "Social Class and
             Children's Reading Preference." **Reading** 5, 2(June
             1971): 3-9.

7.A.1542.   Grimes, Jesse W., and Allinsmith, Wesley. "Compulsivity,
             Anxiety, and School Achievement." **Merrill-Palmer
             Quarterly** 7(October 1961): 247-271.

7.A.1543.   Hanson, Earl, and Robinson, H. Alan. "Reading Readiness
             and Achievement of Primary Grade Children of Different
             Socio-economic Strata." **The Reading Teacher**
             21(October 1967): 52-56, 79.

7.A.1544.   Harrison, Colin. "The Textbook as an Endangered Species:
             The Implications of Economic Decline and Technological
             Advance on the Place of Reading in Learning." **Oxford
             Review of Education** 7, 3(1981): 231-240.

7.A.1545.   Kawakami, A. J., et al. See Section 2.C.69. entry no. 820.

7.A.1546.   Mazurkiewicz, A. J. See Section 4.A. entry no. 1207.

7.A.1547.   McEvedy, Rosanna. "Some Social, Cultural and Linguistic
             Issues in Teaching Reading to Children Who Speak English
             as a Second Language." **Australian Journal of Reading**
             9, 3(August 1986): 139-252.

7.A.1548.   Newman, Anabel P. **Twenty Lives Revisited: A Longitudinal
             Study of the Impact of Literacy on the Occupations and
             Schooling of Students Who Were Low Reading Readiness
             in First Grade (1964-1978), With Special Attention to
             Model, Motivation, Interest, Perseverance, and
             Pressure.** Bloomington, Indiana: Newman, 1980.

7.A.1549.   Osa, O. See Section 2.B.1. entry no. 114.

77A.1550.   Padron, Yolanda N., et al. "Analyzing Bilingual and
             Monolingual Students' Perceptions of Their Reading
             Strategies." **The Reading Teacher** 39, 5(January 1986):
             430-433.

7.A.1551.   Pribic, Rado. "Young People's Literature in the Federal
             Republic of Germany Today." **Journal of Reading** 24,
             4(January 1981): 304-307.

7.A.1552.   Pumfrey, P. D., and Dixon, Elise. "Junior Children's
             Attitudes to Reading." **Reading** 4, 2(June 1970): 19-
             26.

7.A.1553.   "Reading: Old and New." Special Issue. **Daedalus** 112,
             1(Winter 1983): 1-254.

7.A.1554.   Roberts, Donald F., et al. "Reading and Television:
             Predictors of Reading Achievement at Different Age
             Levels." **Communication Research: An International
             Quarterly** 11, 1(January 1984): 9-49.

7.A.1555.   Russell, Jenifer. "Reading Surveys." **Reading** 4, 3
            (December 1970):   13–18.

7.A.1556.   Seitz, Victoria. See Section 4.A. entry no. 1217.

7.A.1557.   Sartain, Harry W. "Research Summary: Family
            Contributions to Reading Attainment." In **Mobilizing
            Family Forces for Worldwide Reading Success**, pp. 4–18.
            Edited by Harry W. Sartain. Newark, Delaware: Inter-
            national Reading Association, 1981.

7.A.1558.   Staiger, Ralph C. and Andresen, Oliver. See Section 2.A.
            entry no. 90.

7.A.1559.   Taiwo, Olande. See Section 2.A. entry no. 95.

7.A.1560.   True, Judith Napier. **A Comparison of Reading Interests
            by Economic Level.** Ann Arbor, Michigan: University
            Microfilms, 1974. Order No. 75–9456. ED 105 399.

B.   LITERACY

7.B.1561.   Allen, Sheilan, and Matheson, Joyce. **The Two Faces of
            Literacy.** Paper presented at the Annual Meeting of
            the International Reading Association, Transmountain
            Regional Conference. Vancouver: n.p., 1977. ED 154
            351.

7.B.1562.   Bormuth, J. R. "Reading Literacy: Its Definition and
            Assessment." **Reading Research Quarterly** 9(1973): 7–
            66.

7.B.1563.   Cooperman, Paul. "The Decline of Literacy." **Journal of
            Communication** 30(Winter 1980): 113–122.

7.B.1564.   Crosby, Muriel. "Reading and Literacy in the Education of
            the Disadvantaged." **The Reading Teacher** 19(October
            1965): 18–22.

7.B.1565.   Downing, John. "An Application of the Comparative Method
            to a Practical Educational Problem: Literacy
            Learning." **School Review** 83, 3(May 1975): 449–459.

7.B.1566.   Downing, John, et al. See Section 2.C.50. entry no. 675.

7.B.1567.   Evans, Peter, and Gleadow, Norman. "Literacy: A Study of
            Literacy Performance and Leisure Activities in
            Victoria, B.C." **Reading-Canada-Lecture** 2, 4(December
            1983): 3–16.

7.B.1568.   Gopinathan, S. "Unfinished Agenda for the 80's: Report
            on International Commitment to Literacy." **The Reading
            Teacher** 35, (January 1982): 430–432.

7.B.1569.   Kozol, Jonathan. See Section 2.C.12. entry no. 240.

7.B.1570.   Lipscombe, R., et al. See Section 2.C.3. entry no. 172.

7.B.1571.   Mabey, Christine. See Section 2.C.17. entry no. 355.

7.B.1572.   O'Halbran, Geroge. See Section 2.B.1. entry no. 113.

7.B.1573.   Ridsdale, Angela; Ryan, D.; and Horan, J., eds. **Literacy for Life.** Proceedings of the Third Australian Reading Conference. Melbourne: Australian Reading Association, 1977.

7.B.1574.   Spolsky, Bernard. **Literacy in the Vernacular: The Navajo Reading Study.** Paper presented at the 69th Annual Meeting of the American Anthropological Association, San Diego, California. November 9, 1970.

7.B.1575.   Vance, Doug. "Research Update: Literacy—Hoax or Hope?" **Wisconsin State Reading Association Journal** 25(October 1980): 24–27.

C. THE DISADVANTAGED

7.C.1576.   Gazean, Sonja, et al. See Section 2.C.9. entry no. 208.

7.C.1577.   Harris, Albert J., et al. See Section 3. entry no. 997.

7.C.1578.   Harris, Albert J., et al. See Section 3. entry no. 998.

7.C.1579.   Lee, Valerie. "Catholic School Minority Students Have 'Reading Proficiency Advantage.'" **Momentum** 17, 3 (September 1986): 20–24.

7.C.1580.   Lloyd, Helene M. See Section 4.D. entry no. 1315.

7.C.1581.   Mills, Queenie B. "The Preschool Disadvantaged Child." In **Reading Disabilities: Selections on Identification and Treatment**, pp. 437–443. Edited by Harold Newman. New York: Odyssey, 1969.

7.C.1582.   Wynn, Sammye J. See Section 4.A. entry no. 1225.

D. INDIGENOUS NORTH AMERICANS

7.D.1583.   Blat, P. "Toward Better Reading for Eskimo Students." **Northian** 9, (Fall 1972): 6–7.

7.D.1584.   Griese, Arnold A. See Section 6.G. entry no. 1451.

7.D.1585.   Hill. Charles H. "A Summer Reading Program with American Indians." **Journal of American Indian Education** 9, 3(May 1970): 10–14.

7.D.1586.   Lankford, Rhonda, and Riley, James D.   "Native American
             Reading Disability." Journal of American Indian
             Education 25, 3(May 1986): 1-11.

7.D.1587.   Markowitz, Alan, et al. See Section 6.E. entry no. 1464.

7.D.1588.   McLaughlin, T. F., et al. "Reading Achievement in the
             Northern Cheyenne Behavior Analysis Model of Follow
             Through." Reading Improvement 19, 2(Summer 1982):
             111-113.

7.D.1589.   McLaughlin, T. F., et al. "Dissemination Efforts of the
             Northern Cheyenne Behavior Analysis Model of Follow
             Through." Reading Improvement 19, 2(Summer 1982):
             149-151.

7.D.1590.   Narang, H. L. "Teaching Indian Children to Read." Query
             12, 3(Fall 1982): 15-24.

7.D.1591.   Philion, William L. E., et al. See Section 2.C.9. entry
             no. 214.

7.D.1592.   Simpson-Tyson, Audrey K. "Are Native American First
             Graders Ready to Read? The Reading Teacher 31, 7
             (April 1978): 798-801.

7.D.1593.   Spolsky, Bernard. See Section 7.B. entry no. 1574.

7.D.1594.   Stensland, Anna L. "American Indian Culture and the Read-
             ing Program." Journal of Reading 15, 1(October 1971):
             22-26.

E. BLACKS

7.E.1595.   Austin, Lettie J. See Section 4.D. entry no. 1292.

7.E.1596.   Barnitz, John G. "Black English and Other Dialects:
             Sociolinguistic Implications for Reading Instruction."
             The Reading Teacher 33, 7(April 1980): 779-786.

7.E.1597.   Boykin, A. Wade. See Section 2.C.69. entry no. 786.

7.E.1598.   Cooper, Bernice. See Section 2.C.69. entry no. 795.

7.E.1599.   Dummett, Leonie. See Section 2.C.69. entry no. 801.

7.E.1600.   Durkin, Dolores. "Poor Black Children Who Are Successful
             Readers: An Investigation." Urban Education 19,
             1(April 1984): 53-76.

7.E.1601.   Mabey, Christine. See Section 2.C.17. entry no. 355.

7.E.1602.   Simons, Herbert D. See Section 4.A. entry no. 1219.

F. RURAL READERS

7.F.1603.   Behrstock, Julian. See Section 4.D. entry no. 1295.

7.F.1604.   Negin, G. A. See Section 2.C.69. entry no. 844.

7.F.1605.   Spencer, Doris U., et al. See Section 3 entry no. 1126.

G. THE THIRD WORLD

7.G.1606.   Bulcock, Jeffrey W., et al. See Section 2.A. entry no. 2.

7.G.1607.   Crawford, Leslie W. "Providing Effective Reading In-
             struction for Refugee Students." **Reading Manitoba**
             3, 2(February 1983): 3-38.

7.G.1608.   Karim, Yaakub Bin. See Section 2.B.8. entry no. 130.

7.G.1609.   King, Kenneth. See Section 2.A. entry no. 56.

7.G.1610.   McSwain, Martha I. B. "Opportunities to Use Family
             Resources for Reading in the Developing Countries of
             Africa." In **Mobilizing Family Forces for Worldwide
             Reading Success**, pp. 19-34. Edited by Harry W.
             Sartain. Newark, Delaware: International Reading
             Association, 1981.

7.G.1611.   Nguyen, Leim T., and Henkin, Alan B. "A Second Generation
             Readability Formula for Vietnamese." **Journal of
             Reading** 29, 3(December 1985): 219-225.

H. MEXICAN-AMERICANS

7.H.1612.   Garcia, Ricardo L. "Mexican Americans Learn Through
             Language Experience." **The Reading Teacher** 28, 3
             (December 1974): 301-305.

7.H.1613.   Hoffer, Kathleen R. "Assessment and Instruction of Read-
             ing Skills: Results with Mexican-American Students."
             Learning Disability Quarterly 6, 4(Fall 1983): 458-
             467.

7.H.1614.   Justin, Neal. "Mexican-American Reading Habits and Their
             Cultural Basis." **Journal of Reading** 16, 6(March
             1973): 467-473.

7.H.1615.   Peterson, Marilyn L. "Mexican-American Children: What Do
             They Prefer to Read?" **Reading World** 22, (December
             1982): 129-131.

7.H.1616.   Robertson, Douglas J., et al. See Section 4.G. entry no.
             1361.

7.H.1617.   Trepper, Terry Steven, and Robertson, Douglas J.   "The
             Effects of I.T.A. on the Reading Achievement of
             Mexican-American Children: A Follow-Up." Reading
             Improvement 12, 3(February 1975):   177-183.

7.H.1618.   Ziros, Gail I.   See Section 2.C.69. entry no. 882.

8

Correlates of the
Organization of Reading

A. CONTENT AREAS

8.A.1619.   Calhoun, Calfey C., et al. See Section 3. entry no. 924.

8.A.1620.   DeBoer, John, and Whipple, Gertrude. "Reading Development
            in Other Curriculum Areas." In **Development in and
            Through Reading**, 60th Yearbook of the NSSE, Part I,
            pp. 54-74. Edited by Paul A. Witty (Chairman).
            Chicago: University of Chicago, 1961.

8.A.1621.   Kincaid, J. Peter, et al. See Section 3. entry no. 1028.

8.A.1622.   Mateja, John A., and Collins, Martha D.   "A Qualitative
            Analysis of Content Area Reading--1930 Revisited."
            Reading Psychology 5, 3-4(1984): 219-233.

8.A.1623.   Mayes, Paul B. See Section 3. entry no. 1056.

8.A.1624.   McNinch, George H. ed. **Reading in the Disciplines**. Second
            Yearbook of the American Reading Forum. Athens,
            Georgia: The American Reading Forum, 1982.

8.A.1625.   Moore, Walter J. "What Does Research in Reading Reveal
            About Reading in the Context Fields?" **English Journal**
            58(May 1969): 707-718.

B. PRIMARY EDUCATION

8.B.1626.   Arthur, Grace. "A Quantitative Study of the Results of
            Grouping First Grade Children According to Mental
            Age." **Journal of Educational Research** 12(October
            1925): 173-185.

8.B.1627.   Austin, Mary C., and Morrison, Coleman. **The First R: The
             Harvard Report on Reading in Elementary Schools.** New
             York: Macmillan, 1963, pp. 73-74.

8.B.1628.   Blom, Gaston E.; Waite, R. R.; and Zimet, S. G. "Content
             of First Grade Reading Books." **The Reading Teacher**
             21(1968):   317-323.

8.B.1629.   Board of Education. **Report of the Consultative Committee
             on the Primary School.** London: H.M.S.O., 1931.

8.B.1630.   Bezeinski, Joseph E.; Harrison, M. Lucile; and McKee,
             Paul. "Should Johnny Read in the Kindergarten?" **The
             Education Digest** 33(October 1967):   44-46.

8.B.1631.   Central Advisory Council. **Children and Their Primary
             Schools.** London: H.M.S.O., 1967.

8.B.1632.   Dykstra, Robert. "Classroom Implications of the First-
             Grade Studies." In **Professional Focus on Reading,**
             Proceedings of the College Reading Association Con-
             ference, Volume 9, pp. 53-59. Edited by Clay A.
             Ketcham. N.P.: n.p., 1968.

8.B.1633.   Dykstra, Robert, and Tinney, Ronald. "Sex Differences in
             Reading Readiness: First Grade Achievement and Second
             Grade Achievement." In **Reading and Realism.** Edited
             by J. Allen Figurel. Newark, Delaware: International
             Reading Association, 1969.

8.B.1634.   Fitzgerald, Thomas P. See Section 2.A. entry no. 22.

8.B.1635.   "Introduction: Primary-School Texts and Teaching Methods
             in the Wake of the Cultural Revolution." See Section
             2.C.10. entry no. 229.

8.B.1636.   "Kindergarten Education, 1967-68." **National Education
             Association Research Bulletin** 47(March 1969):   10-13.

8.B.1637.   Kyostio, O. K. See Section 2.C.20. entry no. 399.

8.B.1638.   Malmquist, Eve. See Section 2.C.63. entry no. 759.

8.B.1639.   McCracken, R. A. "A Two-Year Study of the Reading
             Achievement of Children Who Were Reading When They
             Entered First Grade." **Journal of Educational Research**
             59(1966):   207-210.

8.B.1640.   Morris, J. M. See Section 2.C.17. entry no. 358.

8.B.1641.   Roberts, T. "Frustration Level Reading in the Infant
             School." **Educational Research** 19, (November 1976):
             41-44.

C. MIDDLE SCHOOL/JUNIOR HIGH SCHOOL

8.C.1642.   Chichii, Katsunori. See Section 2.C.36. entry no. 570.

8.C.1643.   Lovell, K. "Informal v. Formal Education and Reading
             Attainments in the Junior School." **Educational
             Research** 6(November 1963): 71-76.

8.C.1644.   Shields, M. See Section 2.C.17. entry no. 382.

D. SECONDARY SCHOOLS

8.D.1645.   Chichii, Katsunori. See Section 2.C.36. entry no. 570.

8.D.1646.   Hafner, Lawrence E. **Improving Reading in Secondary
             Schools.** New York: Macmillan, 1967.

8.D.1647.   Horner, Jim, et al. See Section 2.C.3. entry no. 167.

8.D.1648.   Karlin, Robert. "What Does Research in Reading Reveal
             About Reading and the High School Student?" **English
             Journal** 58(March 1969): 386-395.

8.D.1649.   Marksheffel, Ned D. **Better Reading in the Secondary
             School.** New York: Ronald, 1966.

8.D.1650.   Smith, Nila Banton. "Questions Administrators Ask About
             Reading in the Secondary Schools." In **Corrective
             Reading in the High School Classroom, Perspectives in
             Reading, No. 6,** pp. 114-129. Edited and compiled by
             H. Alan Robinson and Sidney J. Rauch. Newark,
             Delaware: International Reading Association, 1966.

8.D.1651.   Strang, Ruth; McCullough, Constance; and Traxler, Arthur.
             The Improvement of Reading, 4th Edition. New York:
             McGraw-Hill, 1967.

E. HIGHER EDUCATION

8.E.1652.   Hayward, F. M. See Section 2.C.9. entry no. 210.

8.E.1653.   Hennessey, James, and Loveless, Eugene. "The Contribution
             of Three Reading Tests to a Community College Place-
             ment Program." **Educational and Psychological Measure-
             ment** 36, 2(Summer 1976): 459-464.

8.E.1654.   Kaufman, Nancy J., et al. "Awareness of the Use of Compre-
             hension Strategies in Good and Poor College Students."
             Reading Psychology 6, 1-2(1985): 1-11.

8.E.1655.   Kharma, N. N. See Section 2.C.38. entry no. 624.

8.E.1656.   Larsen, Janet J.; Tillman, Chester E.; and Cranney, A.
             Garr. "Trends in College Freshman Reading Ability."

Journal of Reading 19(February 1976):   367–369.

8.E.1657.   Obah, T. Y.   See Section 2.C.46. entry no. 657.

8.E.1658.   Smithies, Michael.   See Section 2.C.50. entry no. 679.

9

Correlates of the Improvement of Reading

A. READING IMPROVEMENT

9.A.1659. Boucherant, Elisabeth. See Section 2.A. entry no. 1.

9.A.1660. Graham, Steve. See Section 3. entry no. 981.

9.A.1661. Harris, Albert J. **How to Increase Reading Ability**, 5th
           Edition. New York: McKay, 1970.

9.A.1662. Strang, Ruth. "Evaluation of Development in and Through
           Reading." In **Measurement and Evaluation of Reading**,
           pp. 35-48. Edited by Roger Farr. New York:
           Harcourt, 1970.

9.A.1663. Whiting, P. R. "Remedial Reading and the Jenny Lamond
           Method." **Forum of Education** 33, 1(March 1974): 58-
           64.

9.A.1664. World Congress on Reading, 3d, Sydney, 1970. **Improving
           Reading Ability Around the World.** Edited by Dorothy
           Kendall Bracken and Eve Malmquist. Newark, Delaware:
           International Reading Association, 1971.

B. READING INTERESTS

9.B.1665. Ellison, Tom, et al. See Section 7.A. entry no. 1541.

9.B.1666. Palmer, Princess A., and Palmer, Barbara C. "Reading
           Interests of Middle School Black and White Students."
           Reading Improvement 20, 2(Summer 1983): 151-155.

9.B.1667. Peterson, Marilyn L. See Section 7.H. entry no. 1615.

9.B.1668. Schofer, Gil. See Section 2.C.17. entry no. 376.

C. PROGRAMS AND PLANNING

9.C.1669.   Allen, James E., Jr. "Target for the 70's." **American
             Education** 5(December 1969): 2-4.

9.C.1670.   Barrett, Thomas C. "Goals of the Reading Program: The
             Basis for Evaluation." In **The Evaluation of
             Children's Reading Achievement, Perspectives in
             Reading,** No. 8, pp. 13-26. Compiled and edited by
             Thomas C. Barrett. Newark, Delaware: International
             Reading Association, 1967.

9.C.1671.   Brignac, Burke, et al. See Section 3. entry no. 917.

9.C.1672.   Freebody, Peter, et al. See Section 2.C.3. entry no. 164.

9.C.1673.   Gephart, William J. "Targeted Research and Development
             Program on Reading--Part II: The Initial Program
             Plan." **American Educational Research Journal** 7
             (May 1970): 435-448.

9.C.1674.   Gonzales, Esperanza A. See Section 2.C.52. entry no. 684.

9.C.1675.   Kerfoot, James F., ed. **First Grade Reading Programs.**
             Newark, Delaware: International Reading Association,
             1967.

9.C.1676.   Stever, L. O., and Steddom, S. S. "From McGuffey to the
             Eighties: American Basic Reading Programs." **Teacher**
             96, (May/June 1979): 58.

9.C.1677.   Ungaro, D. See Section. 2.C.62. entry no. 743.

D. TEACHER PREPARATION

9.D.1678.   Austin, Mary C. "Professional Training of Reading
             Personnel." In **Innovation and Change in Reading
             Instruction,** 67th Yearbook of the NSSE, Part 2, pp.
             357-396. Edited by Helen M. Robinson. Chicago:
             University of Chicago, 1968.

9.D.1679.   Austin, Mary C. "Preparing Teachers and Reading Special-
             ists." In **Current Issues in Reading,** Proceedings of
             the Annual Convention, No. 13, Part 2, pp. 444-451.
             Edited by Nila B. Smith. Newark, Delaware: Inter-
             national Reading Association, 1969.

9.D.1680.   Austin, Mary C., et al. **The Torch Lighters: Tomorrow's
             Teachers of Reading.** Cambridge, Massachusetts:
             Graduate School of Education, Harvard University,
             1961.

9.D.1681.   Downing, John. "The Teacher Variable." In **Comparative
             Reading,** pp. 128-168. Edited by John Downing. New
             York: Macmillan, 1973.

9.D.1682.   Feitelson, Dina. See Section 2.C.33. entry no. 549.

9.D.1683.   Hall, Mary Anne. "Teacher Education in Reading." **The Reading Teacher** 22(December 1968): 265-270.

9.D.1684.   Harris, A. J. "The Effective Teacher of Reading." **The Reading Teacher** 23(December 1969): 195-204, 238.

9.D.1685.   Lowry, William C. "Some Innovations in the Preparation of Teachers." **The Education Digest** 35(February 1969): 28-31.

9.D.1686.   Morris, A., et al. See Section 2.C.3. entry no. 176.

9.D.1687.   Moyle, Donald. See Section 2.C.17. entry no. 362.

9.D.1688.   Professional Standards and Ethics Committee, International Reading Association. **Minimum Standards for Professional Preparation in Reading for Classroom Teachers.** Newark, Delaware: International Reading Association, 1965.

9.D.1689.   Professional Standards and Ethics Committee, International Reading Association. **Minimum Standards for Professional Training of Reading Specialists.** Newark, Delaware: International Reading Association, 1965.

9.D.1690.   Professional Standards and Ethics Committee, International Reading Association. **Reading Specialists: Roles, Responsibilities, and Qualifications.** Newark, Delaware: International Reading Association, 1968.

9.D.1691.   Robinson, H. Alan. "Preparing Teachers of Reading in the United States." **Australian Journal of Reading** 2, 1 (March 1979): 9-17.

9.D.1692.   Smith, Richard J., et al. See Section 4.B. entry no. 1257.

9.D.1693.   Strickland, Ruth G. "A Challenge to Teachers of Reading." **Education Digest** 35, 1(September 1969): 51-54.

E. DIAGNOSIS AND TREATMENT

9.E.1694.   Delacato, C. H. **The Diagnosis and Treatment of Speech and Reading Problems.** Springfield, Illinois: Thomas, 1963.

9.E.1695.   Harris, Albert J. "Diagnosis and Remedial Instruction in Reading." In **Innovation and Change in Reading Instruction,** 67th Yearbook of the NSSE, Part 2, pp. 159-194. Edited by Helen M. Robinson. Chicago: University of Chicago, 1968.

9.E.1696.   McCall, Rozanne A., et al. See Section 3. entry no. 1057.

9.E.1697.   Robinson, Helen M. "Corrective and Remedial Instruction."
            Chapter XX in **Development in and Through Reading,**
            pp. 362-366. 60th Yearbook of the NSSE, Part 1.
            Chicago: University of Chicago, 1961.

9.E.1698.   Rosenberg, M. S. "Error Correction During Oral Reading."
            Learning Disability Quarterly 9(Summer 1986): 182-
            192.

9.E.1699.   Rothman, S. L. "The Poor Reader in the High School:
            Toward a Philosophy of Remedial Reading." **Australian
            Journal of Reading** 4, 3(August 1981): 137-141.

9.E.1700.   Tinker, M. A. "Diagnostic and Remedial Reading."
            Elementary School Journal 33, (December 1932): 293-
            306.

9.E.1701.   Tobin, D., and Pumfrey, P. D. "Some Long Term Effects of
            the Remedial Teaching of Reading." **Educational
            Research** 29, (November 1976): 1-12.

10

Correlates of Evaluation
and Research in Reading

A. EVALUATION

10.A.1702. Ammons, Margaret. "Evaluation: What Is It? Who Does It? When Should It be Done?" In The Evaluation of Children's Reading Achievement, Perspectives in Reading, No. 8, pp. 1-12. Compiled and edited by Thomas C. Barrett. Newark, Delaware: International Reading Association, 1967.

10.A.1703. Anderson, Robert H., and Cynthia Ritsher. "Pupil Progress." In Encyclopedia of Educational Research, 4th Edition, pp. 1050-1062. Edited by Robert L. Ebel. New York: Macmillan, 1969.

10.A.1704. Austin, Mary C.; Bush, C. L.; and Huebner, M. H. Reading Evaluation: Appraisal Techniques for School and Classroom. New York: Ronald, 1961.

10.A.1705. Bloom, Benjamin S., et al. Taxonomy of Educational Objectives, Handbook I, Cognitive Domain. New York: McKay, 1956, p. 119.

10.A.1706. Bookbinder, G. E. "Variations in Reading Test Norms." Educational Research 12(1970): 99-105.

10.A.1707. Buros, Oscar, ed. Reading Tests and Reviews. Highland Park, New Jersey: Gryphon Press, 1968.

10.A.1708. Crispin, Lisa, et al. "The Relevance of Visual Sequential Memory to Reading." British Journal of Educational Psychology 54, 1(February 1984): 24-30.

10.A.1709. de Hirsch, Katrina; Jansky, Jeanette J.; and Langford, William S. Predicting Reading Fortune: A Preliminary Study. New York: Harper, 1966.

10.A.1710. Farr, Roger. "Reading: The Good News and the
            Challenges." The California Reader 1(April 1979):
            23-28.

10.A.1711. Frostig, Marianne, and Horne, David. The Frostig Program
            for the Developmental Test of Perception. Palo Alto,
            California: Consulting Psychologists Press, 1964.

10.A.1712. Fry, Edward. "Reading Rate in 1908." Journal of Reading
            13, 8(May 1970): 593-596.

10.A.1713. Gephart, William J. Application of the Convergence
            Technique to Basic Studies of the Reading Process,
            Final Report. Washington, D.C.: National Center for
            Educational Research and Development, U.S. Office of
            Education, Project 8-0737, 149, 174, 1970.

10.A.1714. Glass, Gene V., and Robbins, Melvyn P. "A Critique of
            Experiments on the Role of Neurological Organization
            in Reading Performance." Reading Research Quarterly
            3(Fall 1967): 5-52.

10.A.1715. Husen, Torsten. See Section 2.A. entry no. 38.

10.A.1716. Johns, Jerry L, and Vacca, Richard T. "An Inquiry into
            Summer Loss in Reading: Grades 1-7." Reading Horizons
            24, 3(Spring 1984): 208-215.

10.A.1717. Johnson, David A., and Wollersheim, Janet P. "A Comparison
            of the Test Performance of Average and Below Average
            Readers on the McCarthy Scales of Childrens'
            Abilities." Journal of Reading Behavior 8, 4(Winter
            1976): 397-403.

10.A.1718. Katz, M. Sex Bias in Educational Testing: A Sociolo-
            gist's Perspective. Paper presented at the Inter-
            national Symposium on Educational Testing. The Hague:
            n.p., 1973.

10.A.1719. Krathwohl, David R.; Bloom, B. S.; and Masia, B. B.
            Taxonomy of Educational Objectives: Handbook II:
            Affective Domain. New York: McKay, 1964.

10.A.1720. Lachat, Mary Ann. See Section 2.C.69. entry no. 826.

10.A.1721. Ministry of Education. Standards of Reading 1948 to 1956.
            Pamphlet No. 32. London: H.M.S.O., 1957.

10.A.1722. Newcomer, Phyllis L. "A Comparison of Two Published
            Reading Inventions." Remedial and Special Education
            6, 1(January-February 1985): 31-36.

10.A.1723. Nicholls, A. "A Second Survey of Reading Tests Used in
            Schools." In Reading: What of the Future?, pp.
            183-191. Edited by Donald Moyle. London: United
            Kingdom Reading Association, 1975.

10.A.1724.   Robinson, Helen M., ed. **Evaluation of Reading.** Supple-
             mentary **Educational Monographs, No. 88.** Chicago:
             University of Chicago, 1958.

10.A.1725.   Shearer, E. "Long-term Effects of Remedial Education."
             Educational Research 9, (June 1967): 219-222.

10.A.1726.   Singer, Martin H., ed. **Competent Reader, Disabled Reader:
             Research and Application.** Hillsdale, New Jersey: L.
             Erlbaum Associates, 1982.

10.A.1727.   "Standards of Reading." **Times Educational Supplement**
             2305:99, July 24, 1959; Discussion 2306:123, July 31,
             1959.

10.A.1728.   Stauffer, Russell G., and Hammond, W. Dorsey. **Effective-
             ness of a Language Arts and Basic Reader Approach to
             First Grade Reading Instruction.** Newark, Delaware:
             University of Delaware, 1965.

10.A.1729.   Tinker, Karen J. "The Role of Laterality in Reading Dis-
             ability." In **Reading and Inquiry,** Proceedings of the
             International Reading Association, pp. 300-303.
             Edited by J. A. Figurel. N.P.: n.p., 1965.

10.A.1730.   Tittle, C. K. **Women and Educational Testing: A Selective
             Review of the Research Literature and Testing
             Practices.** Princeton, New Jersey: Educational
             Testing Service, 1973.

10.A.1731.   Tyler, Ralph W. ed. **Educational Evaluation: New Roles,
             New Means,** 68th Yearbook of the NSSE, Part 2.
             Chicago: University of Chicago, 1969.

10.A.1732.   Young, Beverly S. "A Simple Formula for Predicting
             Reading Potential." **The Reading Teacher** 29, 7(April
             1976): 659-661.

B.   THEORETICAL COMPARATIVE READING

10.B.1733.   Blakey, Janis. "Ashton-Warner's Reading Instruction
             Strategy and Piaget." **Education and Society** 1,
             2(1983): 95-112.

10.B.1734.   Cleland, Craig J. "Learning to Read: Piagetian
             Perspectives for Instruction." **Reading World** 20,
             3(March 1981): 223-224.

10.B.1735.   Cohen, Richard. "Early Reading: The State of the
             Problem." **Prospects** 15, 1(1985): 41-48.

10.B.1736.   Craig, Robert P. "Developing a Philosophy of Reading:
             Piaget and Chomsky." **Reading Horizons** 25, 1(Fall 1984):
             38-42.

10.B.1737. Cromer, W., and Wiener, M. "Reading and Reading
           Difficulty: A Conceptual Analysis." Harvard Edu-
           cational Review 37(1967): 620–643.

10.B.1738. Deadman, Ronald. "Comprehending Comprehension: An
           Existential View of Reading." Reading—Canada—
           Lecture 2, 2(April 1983): 62–69.

10.B.1739. Downing, John. "Bases for Camparison." In Comparative
           Reading, pp. 65–84. Edited by John Downing. New
           York: Macmillan, 1973.

10.B.1740. Downing, John. "Theoretical Overview." Reading 9, 2
           (June 1975): 7–13.

10.B.1741. Favre, Bernard, and Perrenoud, Philippe. "The Teaching of
           Reading: From a Single Methodology to Differentiated
           Approaches." Prospects 15, 1(1985): 87–102.

10.B.1742. Jenkinson, Marion D. "Sources of Knowledge for Theories
           of Reading." Journal of Reading Behavior 1(Winter
           1969): 11–26.

10.B.1743. Miller-Jones, Cindy, and Gallagher, Jeanette McCarthy.
           "Piagetian-based Research in Reading: The Bird Is Out
           of the Cage." Reading-Canada-Lecture 2, 3(October
           1983): 41–47.

10.B.1744. Raven, Ronald J., and Salzer, Richard T. "Piaget and
           Reading Instruction." The Reading Teacher 24, 7
           (April 1971): 630–639.

10.B.1745. Robbins, Melvyn P. "The Delacato Interpretation of Neuro-
           logical Organization." Reading Research Quarterly
           1(Spring 1966): 57–78.

10.B.1746. Shuy, R. W. See Section 2.A. entry no. 89.

10.B.1747. Weaver, Constance. "Of Metaphors and Paradigms: Rejecting
           the "Commonsense" View of Reading." Paper presented at
           the Annual Meeting of the International Reading
           Association. Atlanta: 1984. ED 248 481.

C. COMPARATIVE READING RESEARCH METHODOLOGY

10.C.1748. Downing, John. See Section 7.B. entry no. 1565.

10.C.1749. Heyman, Richard. "Comparative Education from an Ethno-
           methodological Perspective." Comparative Education
           15, 3(October 1979): 241–249.

10.C.1750. Loyd, Brenda H., and Steele, Jeannie L. "Assessment of
           Reading Comprehension: A Comparison of Constructs."
           Reading Psychology 7, 1(1986): 1–10.

D. LITERATURE REVIEWS

10.D.1751.   Ahrendt, K. M.   **Annotated Bibliography in Reading Education.**
Vancouver: University of British Columbia.   Department
of University Extension, 1970.

10.D.1752.   Burke, E., and Lewis, D. G.   "Standards of Reading: A
Critical Review of Some Recent Studies."   Educational
Research 17, (June 1975):   163-174.

10.D.1753.   Clymer, Theodore.   "Research in Corrective Reading: Find-
ings, Problems, and Observations."   In **Corrective
Reading in the Elementary Classroom, Perspectives in
Reading, No. 7,** pp. 1-10.   Compiled and edited by
M.S. Johnson, and R. A. Kress.   Newark, Delaware:
International Reading Association, 1967.

10.D.1754.   Davis, F. B.   "Research in Comprehension in Reading."
Reading Research Quarterly 3(1968):   499-545.

10.D.1755.   Dillingofski, Mary Sue.   "Sociolinguistics and Reading:
A Review of the Literature."   **The Reading Teacher**
33, 3(December 1979):   307-312.

10.D.1756.   Ely, Donald P., ed.   "Research Abstracts."   Education
Communication and Technology Journal 31, (Fall 1983):
182-184.

10.D.1757.   Haynes, C. S.   "Annotated Bibliography of the Language
Experience Approach to Reading Instruction."   Contemporary Education 40, (February 1969):   212-224.

10.D.1758.   Kamil, Michael L., and Moe, Alden, J., eds.   **Perspectives
on Reading Research and Instruction.**   Twenty-Nineth
Yearbook of the National Reading Conference.
Washington, D.C.: The National Reading Conference,
1980.

10.D.1759.   Manheim, Theodore, et al.   **Sources in Educational
Research.   A Selected and Annotated Bibliography;
Volume I: Parts I-X.**   Detroit: Wayne State
University Press, 1969.   ED 032 753.

10.D.1760.   Page, William, and Moore, David.   "Significant Research in
Reading: 1960-1980."   **The New England Reading
Association Journal** 17, 3(Autumn 1982):   35-43.

10.D.1761.   Sheridan, E. Marcia.   See Section 4.C. entry no. 1284.

10.D.1762.   Spache, George D.   **Classroom Organization for Reading
Instruction: An Annotated Bibliography.**   Newark,
Delaware: International Reading Association, 1965.

10.D.1763.   Summers, E. G., Courtney, L.; and Edwards, P., comps.
"Guides to Professional Textbooks and Research in

Secondary Reading Instruction." The English Quarterly
7, (Summer 1974): 124-146.

10.D.1764. Teale, W. H. Early Reading: A Comprehensive Annotated
Bibliography. Bundoora, Victoria: La Trobe University.
Centre for the Study of Curriculum and Teacher
Education, 1979.

10.D.1765. Tebble, Helen A. "Bibliography of Research in Reading in
Australia." Reading Education 2, (Autumn 1977): 41-
62.

10.D.1766. Tinker, M. A. See Section 9.E. entry no. 1700.

10.D.1767. Venezky, R. L. Basic Studies on Reading. N.P.: Levin
and Williams, 1970.

10.D.1768. Vernon, M. D. Backwardness in Reading. London:
Cambridge University Press, 1957.

E. COMPARATIVE READING RESEARCH

10.E.1769. Anastasi, A. "On the Formation of Psychological Traits."
American Psychologist 25(1970): 899-910.

10.E.1770. Brimer, M. Alan. "Methodological Problems of Research."
In Comparative Reading, pp. 13-31. Edited by John
Downing. Macmillan, 1973.

10.E.1771. Clymer, Theodore. "What is 'Reading'?: Some Current
Concepts." In Innovation and Change in Reading
Instruction, 67th Yearbook of the NSSE, Part 2, pp.
7-29. Edited by Helen M. Robinson. Chicago:
University of Chicago, 1968.

10.E.1772. Cooper, Rayna. "The Nelson-Denny Reading Test: A
Comparison." Journal of Developmental and Remedial
Education 6, spec. issu. (1983): 18-19.

10.E.1773. Farr, Robert, and Tone, Bruce. "What Does Research Show?"
Today's Education 67(November-December 1978): 33-36.

10.E.1774. Feitelson, Dina. See Section 2.A. entry no. 21.

10.E.1775. Groebel, Lillian. See Section 2.C.17. entry no. 332.

10.E.1776. Guthrie, John T. "Research: Classrooms and Battalions."
Journal of Reading 24, 4(January 1981): 364-366.

10.E.1777. Hallgren, B. Specific Dyslexia: A Clinical and Genetic
Study. Copenhagen: Munksgaard, 1950.

10.E.1778. Hinshelwood, J. Congenital Word Blindness. London:
Lewis, 1917.

10.E.1779. Malmquist, Eve. "A Decade of Reading Research in Europe,
            1959-1969: A Review". Journal of Educational Re-
            search 63, 7(1970): 309-329.

10.E.1780. Rabinovitch, R., et al. "A Research Approach to Reading
            Retardation." Research Publication of the Association
            for Research in Nervous and Mental Disease 34(1954):
            363-396.

10.E.1781. Seidenfaden, F. "Some Thoughts on the Function of
            Comparative Education in the Context of Educational
            Research." Comparative Education 8, 1(April 1972):
            31-41.

10.E.1782. Sheldon, Susan A. "Comparison of Two Teaching Methods for
            Reading Comprehension." Journal of Research in Reading
            7, 1(February 1984): 41-52.

10.E.1783. Smith, Cyrus F., Jr., and Harrison, Margaret Drumm. "A
            Comparative Analysis of Three Widely Used Graded Word
            Reading Tests." Paper presented at the Annual Meeting
            of the Great Lakes Regional International Reading
            Association. Springfield, Illinois: 1983. ED 235
            473.

10.E.1784. Thomson, M. "Laterality and Reading Attainment." The
            British Journal of Educational Psychology 45, (November
            1975): 317-321.

10.E.1785. Valtin, Renate. "Dyslexia: Deficit In Reading or Deficit
            in Research?" Reading Research Quarterly 14, 2(1978-
            1979): 201-221.

10.E.1786. Weintraub, Samuel. "Two Significant Trends in Reading
            Research." In Reading and Writing Instruction in the
            United States: Historical Trends. Edited by H. Alan
            Robinson. Urbana, Illinois: ERIC Clearinghouse on
            Reading and Communication Skills, 1977: Newark,
            Delaware: International Reading Association, 1977.

F. READING READINESS

10.F.1787. Downing, J. A. "Is a Mental Age of Six Essential for
            Reading Readiness?" Educational Research 6, (November
            1963): 16-28.

10.F.1788. Dystrak, Robert, et al. See Section 8.B. entry no. 1633.

10.F.1789. Thackray, Derek V. See Section 3. entry no. 1138.

G. GROUPING RESEARCH

10.G.1790. Bradfield, R. H. "Academic Achievement: Then and Now."
            Academic Therapy 5(1970): 259-265.

10.G.1791. Browning, Ellen R. See Section 3. entry no. 920.

10.G.1792. Spache, George D. See Section 10.D. entry no. 1762.

H. SEX DIFFERENCES

10.H.1793. Ansara, Alice, et al. eds. **Sex Differences in Dyslexia.**
            Townson, Maryland: The Orton Dyslexia Society, 1981.

10.H.1794. Brimer, M. A. See Section 3. entry no. 918.

10.H.1795. Dwyer, Carol Anne. See Section 3. entry no. 959.

10.H.1796. Dwyer, Edward J. See Section 3. entry no. 960.

10.H.1797. Dykstra, Robert, et al. See Section 8.B. entry no. 1633.

10.H.1798. Gross, Alice Dzen. See Section 2.C.33. entry no. 553.

10.H.1799. Hogrebe, Mark C., et al. "Are There Gender Differences in
            Reading Achievement? An Investigation Using the High
            School and Beyond Data." **Journal of Educational
            Psychology** 77, 6(December 1985): 716-724.

10.H.1800. Johnson, Dale D. **An Investigation of Sex Differences in
            Reading in Four English Speaking Nations.** Madison,
            Wisconsin: Research and Development Center for
            Cognitive Learning, 1972.

10.H.1801. Johnson, Dale D. See Section 2.A. entry no. 48.

10.H.1802. Kagan, J. "The Child's Sex Role Classification of School
            Objects." **Child Development** 35(1964): 1051-1056.

10.H.1803. Kalamazoo, Michigan. Board of Education. Committee to
            Study Sex Discrimination in the Kalamazoo Public
            Schools. **Sex Discrimination in an Elementary Reading
            Program: A Report Based on the Work of the Committee
            to Study Sex Discrimination in the Kalamazoo Public
            Schools.** Lansing, Michigan: Michigan Women's Com-
            mission, 1974.

10.H.1804. Klein, Howard A. "What Effect Does Non-Sexist Content
            Have on the Reading of Boys and Girls." **Reading
            Improvement** 16, 2(Summer 1979): 134-138.

10.H.1805. Labercane, G., and Shapiro, J. "Gender Differences in
            Reading: Sociocultural vs. Neurological Influences."
            Reading Improvement 23(Summer 1986): 82-89.

10.H.1806. Riding, R.J., and Cowley, J. "Extraversion and Sex
            Differences in Reading Performance in Eight Year Old
            Children." **British Journal of Educational Psychology**
            56, 1(February 1986): 88-94.

10.H.1807.   "Sex Differences in Reading Words." **Science News** 107,
              11(March 1975): 166-167.

10.H.1808.   Sheridan, E. Marcia. See Section 4.C. entry no. 1284.

10.H.1809.   Tollefson, Nona, et al. "Predicting Reading Achievement
              for Kindergarten Boys and Girls." **Psychology in the
              Schools** 22, 1(January 1985): 34-39.

10.H.1810.   Wood, R. "Sex Differences in Answers to English Language
              Comprehension Items." **Educational Studies** 4(June
              1978): 263-276.

I.   READING ACHIEVEMENT

10.I.1811.   Ahmann, J. Stanley. "Differential Changes in Levels of
              Achievement for Students in Three Age Groups."
              Educational Studies 10(Spring 1979): 35-51.

10.I.1812.   Bates, Gary W. "Developing Reading Strategies for the
              Gifted: A Research Based Approach." **Journal of
              Reading** 27, 7(April 1984): 590-593.

10.I.1813.   Cooper, Bernice. "An Analysis of Reading Achievement of
              White and Negro Pupils in Certain Public Shools in
              Georgia." **School Review** 72(Winter 1962): 462-471.

10.I.1814.   Cox, Theo. "A Follow-Up Study of Reading Attainment in a
              Sample of Eleven-Year Old Disadvantaged Children."
              Educational Studies 5(March 1979): 53-60.

10.I.1815.   Elligett, Jane, et al. See Section 3. entry no. 963.

10.I.1816.   Freebody, Peter, and Tirre, William C. "Achievement Out-
              comes of Two Reading Programmes: an Instance of
              Aptitude--Treatment Interaction." **British Journal of
              Educational Psychology** 55, 1(February 1985): 53-60.

10.I.1817.   Gates, Arthur Irving. See Section 3. entry no. 975.

10.I.1818.   Kershner, John. "Cerebral Dominance in Disabled Readers,
              Good Readers, and Gifted Children: Search for a Valid
              Model." **Child Development** 48, 1(March 1977): 61-67.

10.I.1819.   Krein, Evelyn L., and Zaharias, Jane Ann. "Analysis of
              Able and Disabled Sixth-Grade Readers' Knowledge of
              Story Structure: A Comparison." **Reading Horizons**
              27, 1(Fall 1986): 45-53.

10.I.1820.   McCracken, R. A. "A Two-Year Study of the Reading Achieve-
              ment of Children Who Were Reading When They Entered
              Frist Grade." **Journal of Educational Research** 59
              (1966): 207-210.

10.I.1821.   Phillips, Leonard W., and Bianchi, William W.
             "Desegregation, Reading Achievement and Problem
             Behavior in Two Elementary Schools." Urban Education
             9, 4(January 1975): 325-329.

10.I.1822.   Postelthwaite, T. N. "Success and Failure in School."
             Prospects 10, 3(1980): 249-263.

10.I.1823.   Sartain, Harry W. See Section 7.A. entry no. 1557.

10.I.1824.   Tollefson, Nona, et al. See Section 10.H. entry no. 1809.

10.I.1825.   Walberg, Herbert J. "Correlates of Reading Achievement and
             Attitude: A National Assessment Study." Journal of
             Educational Research 78, 3(January/February 1985):
             159-167.

J. READING DISABILITY

10.J.1826.   Bereiter, Carl, and Englemann, Siegfried. Teaching Dis-
             advantaged Children in the Preschool. Englewood
             Cliffs, New Jersey: Prentice-Hall, 1966.

10.J.1827.   Blanchard, P. "Attitudes and Education in Disabilities."
             Mental Hygiene 13(1929): 550-563.

10.J.1828.   Blanchard, P. "Psychogenic Factors in Some Cases of Read-
             ing Disability." American Journal of Orthopsychiatry
             5(1935): 361-374.

10.J.1829.   Critchley, M. Developmental Dyslexia. London:
             Heinemann, 1964.

10.J.1830.   Critchley, M. The Dyslexic Child. London: Heinemann,
             1970.

10.J.1831.   Cromer, W., et al. See Section 10.B. entry no. 1737.

10.J.1832.   Delacato, C. H. The Treatment and Prevention of Reading
             Problems. Springfield, Illinois: Thomas, 1959.

10.J.1833.   Delacato, C. H. Neurological Organization and Reading.
             Springfield, Illinois: Thomas, 1966.

10.J.1834.   Dunsing, Jack D., and Kephart, N. C. "Motor Generali-
             zations in Space and Time." In Learning Disorders,
             I, pp. 77-121. Edited by Jerome Hellmuth. Seattle,
             Washington: Special Child Publications, 1965.

10.J.1835.   Eaves, June. See Section 7.A. entry no. 1539.

10.J.1836.   Elkin, J. See Section 2.C.3. entry no. 163.

10.J.1837.   Gann, E. Reading Difficulty and Personality Organization.
             New York: King's Crown Press, 1945.

10.J.1838.   Gates, Arthur I., et al.   See Section 4.A. entry no. 1195.

10.J.1839.   Geschwind, N.   "Disconnection Syndromes in Animal and
                   Man."   Brain 88(1956):   585-644.

10.J.1840.   Gunderson, Doris V.   "Reading Problems: Glossary of Term-
                   inology."   Reading Research Quarterly 4(Summer 1969):
                   535-547.

10.J.1841.   Hallgren, B.   See Section 10.E. entry no. 1777.

10.J.1842.   Harber, Jean R.   See Section 3. entry no. 994.

10.J.1843.   Harris, Theodore L.   "Reading."   In Encyclopedia of
                   Educational Research, 4th Edition, pp. 1069-1104.
                   Edited by Robert L. Ebel.   New York: Macmillan, 1969.

10.J.1844.   Isom, John B.   "Some Neuropsychological Findings in
                   Children with Reading Problems."   In The 32nd Year-
                   book of the Claremont College Reading Conference, pp.
                   188-198.   Edited by Malcolm P. Douglass.   Claremont,
                   California: Claremont Reading Conference, 1968.

10.J.1845.   Johnson, Barbara, et al.   "The Debate Over Learning
                   Disability vs. Reading Disability: A Survey of
                   Practioners' Populations and Remedial Methods."
                   Learning Disability Quarterly 6, 3(Summer 1983):   258-
                   264.

10.J.1846.   Kephart, Newell C.   The Slow Learner in the Classroom,
                   2nd Edition.   Columbus, Ohio: Merrill, 1971.

10.J.1847.   Malmquist, Eve, and Valtin, R.   Forderung Legasthenischer
                   Kinder in Der Schule.   Weinheim: n.p., 1974.

10.J.1848.   Measzinni, Paolo.   "Reading Errors: Assessment and
                   Behavioral Intervention."   School Psychology Inter-
                   national 6, 1(January/March 1985):   34-38.

10.J.1849.   Missildine, W.   "The Emotional Background of Thirty
                   Children With Reading Disability."   Nervous Child
                   5(1946):   263-272.

10.J.1850.   Money, John.   "Dyxlexia, A Post Conference Review."   In
                   Reading Disability: Progress and Research Needs in
                   Dyslexia.   Edited by John Money.   Baltimore, Maryland:
                   Johns Hopkins Press, 1962.

10.J.1851.   Monroe, M.   Children Who Cannot Read.   Chicago:
                   University of Chicago Press, 1932.

10.J.1852.   Morsink, Catherine, et al.   "How Disabled Readers Try to
                   Remember Words."   Reading Horizons 188, 3(Spring
                   1978):   174-180.

10.J.1853. Mosse, Hilde L. The Complete Handbook of Children's
            Reading Disorders, Volumes 1 and 2. New York: Human
            Sciences Press, Inc., 1982.

10.J.1854. Mountcastle, V. Interhemispheric Relation and Cerebral
            Dominance. Baltimore, Maryland: Johns Hopkins Press,
            1962.

10.J.1855. Orton, S. "Word Blindness in School Children." Archives
            in Neurology and Psychiatry 14(1925): 581-615.

10.J.1856. Rabinovitch, Ralph D. "Dyslexia: Psychiatric Considera-
            tions." In Reading Disability: Progress and Research
            Needs in Dyslexia, pp. 73-79. Edited by John Money.
            Baltimore, Maryland: Johns Hopkins Press, 1962.

10.J.1857. Sachs, Arlene. "The Effects of Three Prereading
            Activities on Learning Disabled Students: Reading
            Comprehension." Learning Disability Quarterly 6,
            3(Summer 1983): 248-251.

10.J.1858. Sakamoto, Ichiro. See Section 2.C.36. entry no. 602.

10.J.1859. Shiach, G. M. See Section 4.C. entry no. 1285.

10.J.1860. Singer, Martin H. See Section 10.A. entry no. 1726.

10.J.1861. Smith, D. E. P., and Carrigan, Patricia. The Nature of
            Reading Disability. New York: Harcourt, 1959.

10.J.1862. Soderbergh, Ragnhild. "Early Reading with Deaf Children."
            Prospects 15, 1(1985): 77-86.

10.J.1863. Tarnopol, Lester, et al. See Section 3. entry no. 1136.

10.J.1864. Tulchin, S. "Emotional Factors in Reading Disabilities in
            School Children." Journal of Educational Psychology
            26(1935): 443-454.

10.J.1865. Voeller, K. K. S., and Armus, J. "A Comparision of Reading
            Strategies in Genetic Dyslexics and Children with
            Right and Left Brain Deficits. Annals of Dyslexia 36
            (1986): 270-286.

10.J.1866. Western Australia Council for Special Education. See
            Section 2.C.3. entry no. 190.

K. LONGITUDINAL RESEARCH

10.K.1867. Barik, Henri C.; Swain, Merrill; and Gaudino, Vincent A.
            "A Canadian Experiment in Bilingual Schooling in the
            Senior Grades: The Peel Study Through Grade 10."
            Revue Internationale de Psychologie Appliquee 25
            (October 1976): 99-113.

10.K.1868.   Eurich, Alvin C.   "Student Readers: The 50-Year
             Difference."   Change 12(April 1980):   13-15.

10.K.1869.   Greaney, Vincent, et al.   See Section 3. entry no. 984.

10.K.1870.   Newman, Anabel P.   See Section 7.A. entry no. 1548.

10.K.1871.   Tuinman, Jaap.   "Research: Lives Revisited [re. lack of
             longitudinal studies on reading].   Reading--Canada--
             Lecture 1, 4(May 1982):   68-70.

10.K.1872.   Wolf, Maryanne, et al.   "Automaticity, Retrieval
             Processes, and Reading: A Longitudinal Study in
             Average and Impaired Readers."   Child Development 57,
             4(August 1986):   988-1000.

11

Correlates of the Psychology
of Comparative Reading

11.1873. Belikova, A. V. See Section 2.C.62. entry no. 719.

11.1874. Biyin, Zhang. See Section 2.C.10. entry no. 221.

11.1875. Blanchard, P. See Section 10.J. entry no. 1828.

11.1876. Clarke, Desmond. "Reading Acquisition: A Cognitive
          Perspective." **Caribbean Journal of Education** 10,
          1(1983): 45-54.

11.1877. Clay, M. M. **Reading: The Pattern of Complex Behavior.**
          Aukland, New Zealand: Heinemann, 1972.

11.1878. Downing, John, and Leong, Che Kan. **The Psychology of
          Reading.** New York: Macmillan, 1982.

11.1879. Evans, James R., and Smith, Linda Jones. "Psycho-
          linguistic Skills of Early Readers." **The Reading
          Teacher** 30, 1(October 1976): 39-43.

11.1880. Gann, E. See Section 10.J. entry no. 1837.

11.1881. Huey, E. G. See Section 4.B. entry no. 1246.

11.1882. Khokhlova, N. A. See Section 2.C.62. entry no. 732.

11.1883. Missildine, W. See Section 10.J. entry no. 1849.

11.1884. Rabinovitch, Ralph D. See Section 10.J. entry no. 1856.

11.1885. Schonell, F. J. See Section 4.B. entry no. 1255.

11.1886. Tulchin, S. See Section 10.J. entry no. 1864.

12

Correlates of General Reading

A. GENERAL READING

12.A.1887.   Austin, Gilbert R., and Garber, Herbert, eds. The
             Rise and Fall of National Test Scores. New York:
             Academic Press, 1982.

12.A.1888.   Bessell-Brown, Thelma, et al., eds. Reading Into the
             80's. Adelaide: Australian Reading Association,
             1980.

12.A.1889.   Brogan, Peggy, et al. See Section 4.A. entry no. 1179.

12.A.1890.   Burns, D.; Campbell, A.; and Jones, R., eds. Reading,
             Writing and Multiculturalism. Adelaide: Australian
             Reading Association, 1982.

12.A.1891   Burton, William D. Reading in Child Development. New
             York: Bobbs, 1956, p. 528.

12.A.1892.   Chall, J. S. See Section 4.A. entry no. 1183.

12.A.1893.   Chapman, L. John, ed. The Reader and the Text. London:
             Heinemann Educational Books Ltd., 1981.

12.A.1894.   Douglass, Malcolm P., ed. Claremont Reading Conference
             Forty-Sixth Yearbook. Claremont, California:
             Claremont Reading Conference, 1982.

12.A.1895.   Downing, John. Letter in the Correspondence Column.
             Times Educational Supplement (October 13, 1968).

12.A.1896.   Downing, John. "The Meaning of Reading." Reading
             6(1972): 30-33.

12.A.1897. Downing, John. "Other Extraneous Factors." In
            Comparative Reading, pp. 169-180. Edited by John
            Downing. New York: Macmillan, 1973.

12.A.1898. Downing, John. "Some Curious Paradoxes in Reading
            Research." Reading 8-9(1974-75): 2-10.

12.A.1899. Figurel, J. Allen, ed. Reading and Realism. Newark,
            Delaware: International Reading Association, 1969.

12.A.1900. Gagg, J. C. See Section 4.B. entry no. 1243.

12.A.1901. Gates, Arthur I. "The Nature of the Reading Process." In
            Reading in the Elementary School, 48th Yearbook of
            the NSSE, Part II. Chicago: University of Chicago,
            1949.

12.A.1902. Gibson, Eleanor J. Principles of Perceptual Learning and
            Development. New York: Appleton, 1969.

12.A.1903. Gray, W. S. See Section 4.B. entry no. 1244.

12.A.1904. Greaney, Vincent, ed. Studies in Reading. Dublin: The
            Educational Company, 1977.

12.A.1905. Guthrie, John T. "Research: Functional Reading: One or
            Many?" Journal of Reading 22, 7(April 1979): 648-
            650.

12.A.1906. Harris, Theodore L., and Hodges, Richard E., eds. A
            Dictionary of Reading. Newark, Delaware: Inter-
            national Reading Association, 1981.

12.A.1907. Hillerich, Robert L. "Reading: How Are We Doing?" Ohio
            Reading Teacher 12(October 1977): 5-7.

12.A.1908. Hunt, James McVicker. Intelligence and Experience. New
            York: Ronald, 1961.

12.A.1909. Kemp, M. "Assessment of Early Reading." In Acquisition
            of Basic Skills in Early School Years, pp. 66-72.
            Canberra: National Council of Independent Schools,
            1982.

12.A.1910. MacKinnon, G. E., and Waller, T. Gary, eds. Reading
            Research: Advances in Theory and Practice, Vol. 2.
            New York: Academic Press, 1981.

12.A.1911. Maxwell, James. "Towards a Definition of Reading." Read-
            ing 8-9(1974-75): 5-12.

12.A.1912. McNinch, George H., ed. Comprehension: Process and
            Product. First Yearbook of the American Reading
            Forum. Athens, Georgia: The American Reading Forum,
            1981.

12.A.1913. Miller, G. A. "The Magical Number Seven, Plus or Minus
            Two: Some Limits of Our Capacity for Processing
            Information." **Psychological Review** 63(1956): 81–97.

12.A.1914. Moyle, Donald. "Reading: What of the Future?" In
            Reading: What of the Future? pp. 8–13. Edited by
            Donald Moyle. London: United Kingdom Reading
            Association, 1975.

12.A.1915. Newman, Arthur J. "Some Fundamental Oversights." NASSP
            Bulletin 62, 420(October 1978): 12–9.

12.A.1916. Pearson, P. David, and Hansen, Jane, eds. "Reading:
            Disciplined Inquiry in Process and Practice." **Twenty-
            seventh Yearbook of the National Reading Conference,**
            1978.

12.A.1917. "Reading: Old and New." See Section 7.A. entry no. 1553.

12.A.1918. "Reading, Writing, Thinking." Special Issue. **The Reading
            Teacher** 39, 8(April 1986):

12.A.1919. Schubert, Delwyne G. **A Dictionary of Terms and Concepts in
            Reading.** Springfield, Illinois: Thomas, 1964.

12.A.1920. Shuppan, Kagaku Kenkyu-sho. See Section 2.C.36. entry
            no. 615.

12.A.1921. Smith, Frank. **Understanding Reading.** New York: Holt,
            1971.

12.A.1922. Smith, Nila B. "The Future of Reading." In **Reading
            Instruction: An International Forum.** Edited by
            Marion D. Jenkinson. Newark, Delaware: International
            Reading Association, 1967.

12.A.1923. Staiger, Ralph C., et al. See Section 2.A. entry no. 90.

12.A.1924. Strang, Ruth. "The Nature of Reading." In **Problems in
            the Improvement of Reading,** 2nd Edition. Edited by
            Ruth Strang, Constance M. McCullough and Arthur E.
            Traxler. New York: McGraw-Hill, 1955.

12.A.1925. "The Teaching of Reading." See Section 4.A. entry no. 1223.

12.A.1926. Thompson, W. Warren. "Environmental Effects on
            Educational Performance." **Alberta Journal of
            Educational Research** 31, 1(March 1985): 11–25.

12.A.1927. **Yearbook. Claremont Reading Conference.** Claremont,
            California: Clarement Reading Conference, 1985.

B. GENERAL COMPARATIVE READING

12.B.1928. Beardsley, Gillian,· and Wright, Elizabeth. "Comparative

Reading." **Reading** 8-9(1974-75):   27-32.

12.B.1929. Downing, John. "The Future of Comparative Reading." In
            Comparative Reading, pp. 244-256. Edited by John
            Downing. New York: Macmillan, 1973.

12.B.1930. Downing, John. "The Rationale and Scope of Comparative
            Reading." In **Comparative Reading**, pp. 3-12. Edited
            by John Downing. New York: Macmillan, 1973.

12.B.1931. Downing, John. "The Value of Comparative Reading." In
            Handbook on Comparative Reading, pp. 1-7. Edited by
            Eve Malmquist. Newark, Delaware: International Read-
            ing Association, 1982.

12.B.1932. Downing, John, ed. **Comparative Reading**. New York:
            Macmillan, 1973.

12.B.1933. Duke, B. C. "Why Noriko Can Read! Some Hints for
            Johnny." Edcuational Forum 41, 229-236; Reply,
            N.V. Overly 228, January 1977.

12.B.1934. Goodacre, Elizabeth J. **Reading Research 1977**. Reading,
            Berkshire: Centre for the Teaching of Reading,
            University of Reading, 1977.

12.B.1935. Goodacre, Elizabeth J. **Reading Research Review 1978**.
            Reading, Berkshire: University of Reading, 1978.

12.B.1936. Goodacre, Elizabeth J. **Reading Research Review 1979**.
            Reading, Berkshire: University of Reading School of
            Education, 1979.

12.B.1937. Goodacre, Elizabeth J. **Reading Research Review 1980**.
            Reading, Berkshire: University of Reading School of
            Education, 1980.

12.B.1938. Goodacre, Elizabeth J. **Reading Research Review 1981**.
            Reading, Berkshire: University of Reading School of
            Education, 1981.

12.B.1939. Goodacre, Elizabeth J. **Reading Research Review 1982**.
            Reading, Berkshire: University of Reading School of
            Education, 1982.

12.B.1940. Goodacre, Elizabeth J. **Reading Research Review 1983**.
            Reading, Berkshire: University of Reading School of
            Education, 1984.

12.B.1941. Loyd, Brenda H., et al. See Section 10.C. entry no. 1750.

12.B.1942. Malmquist, Eve, ed. **Handbook on Comparative Reading**.
            Newark, Delaware: International Reading Association,
            1982.

12.B.1943. Newcomer, Phyllis L. See Section 10.A. entry no. 1722.

12.B.1944. Redgwell, Laura. "A Comparison of the Traditional and
            Psycholinguistic Approach to Reading." **Manitoba
            Association of Resource Teachers Journal** 3, 5(May
            1984): 15-17.

12.B.1945. Sullivan, Joanna. "Comparing Strategies of Good and Poor
            Comprehenders." **Journal of Reading** 21, 8(May 1978):
            710-715.

12.B.1946. Tuman, Myron C. "A Comparative Review of Reading and
            Listening Comprehension." **Query** 11, 2(May 1981): 39-
            43.

12.B.1947. Wooden, S. L., and Pettibone, T. J. "A Comparative Study
            of Three Beginning Reading Programs for the Spanish
            Speaking Child." **Journal of Reading Behavior** 5, 3
            (Summer 1973): 192-199.

Author Index

Holdaway, D., 647
Holland, Seamans, 525
Hollingsworth, Paul M., 1383
Holmes, Betty C., 1004
Hong, Woong Sun, 715
Hood, Joyce, 36, 238, 1005
Hopkins, Elaine, 729
Horan, J., 1573
Horikawa, Naoyoshi, 574
Horne, David, 1711
Horner, Barbara, 924
Horner, Jim, 167, 1007, 1647
Horner, Peter, 340
Horton, T. R., 886
Horvath, A., 497
Hotyat, Fernand, 25
Howes, Virgil M., 1298
Huck, Charlotte S., 879
Hudson, Jean, 341
Huebner, M. H., 1236, 1704
Huelsman, Charles B., Jr., 1519
Huey, E. B., 1246, 1881
Hughes, Theone, 342, 814
Hummel, Jeffrey W., 211
Hunt, James McVicker, 1908
Hunt, Lyman C., Jr., 1273
Hunter, William J., 212, 1008
Hunter-Grundin, Elizabeth, 343
Husen, Torsten, 37-40, 815, 1009-11, 1715
Huus, Helen, 1312
Hynd, Cynthia R., 1340

Illes, Sander, 498
Imura, T., 1498
Ingham, Jennie, 344
Inner London Education Authority, 345
Institute of International Studies, 513, 546, 892
International Association for the Evaluation of Educational Achievement, 41, 42, 43, 44, 45, 46, 1013-1017, 1486
International Bureau of Education, 422, 1247, 1279
International Conference on Public Education, 1223, 1925
International Education Yearbook, 419
International Institute for Adult Literary Methods, 515
International Reading Association, 434, 541, 903, 1416, 1481, 1487,

1495, 1664, 1688-90
Irvine, D. G., 346
Isaac, Stephen, 816
Ishii, Masako, 601
Isom, John B., 1844

Jackson, J., 168
Jacobson, Milton, D., 996
James, Sybil L., 659
Jansen, M., 253-63, 1248, 1479-80
Jansky, Jeanette J., 1709
Janson, Anne-Jeanette, 1203
Jantzen, J. M., 448
January, G. R., 169, 1274
Jenkinson, Marion D., 47, 1742
Jennings-Wray, Zelleynne, 567
Jiang, Shanye, 230
Jones, Ben, 1047
Jones, D., 170
Jones, Earl, 52
Jones, J. K., 349-50
Jones, R. 1890
Jordan, R. R., 111, 117
Johns, E., 347
Johns, Jerry L., 1018-19, 1419, 1716
Johnson, Barbara, 1845
Johnson, Dale D., 48-50, 1020-21, 1800-01
Johnson, David A., 1717
Johnson, J. David, 51
Johnson, Joseph C., II, 1022
Johnson, Lynne M., 817, 1023
Johnson, Marjorie S., 1024
Johnson, R. D., 1200
Johnson, Terry D., 348, 818
Junge, Barbara, 635
Justin, Neal, 1614

Kachurin, M. G., 730, 731
Kaga, Hideo, 582, 583, 611, 612
Kagan, J., 1802
Kainz, Friedrich, 449
Kalamazoo, Michigan. Board of Education, 819, 1803
Kamavas, Istvan, 499
Kamei, Michiko, 600
Kamil, Michael L., 1758
Kandel, I. L., 420
Karim, Yaakub Bin, 130, 1608
Karlin, Robert, 1648
Karlsen, Bjorn, 53, 1025

Subject Index

About the Compilers

JOHN HLADCZUK and WILLIAM ELLER are members of the
Department of Learning and Instruction at the State University
of New York at Buffalo.